at maimonides table

this book is dedicated
to the unborn dead

at maimonides table

by

philip kuhn

God writes straight with crooked lines
[Portuguese proverb]

And in my going out to meet you
I found you coming towards me
[Jehuda Halevi]

Shearsman Books
Exeter

Published in the United Kingdom in 2009 by
Shearsman Books Ltd
58 Velwell Road
Exeter EX4 4LD

ISBN 978-1-84861-020-0

Second revised edition.

Copyright © philip kuhn, 2009.

The right of philip kuhn to be identified as the author of this work has been asserted by him in accordance with the Copyrights, Designs and Patents Act of 1988. All rights reserved.

acknowledgements
An earlier version of *at maimonides table* was first published in a limited edition by itinerant press, Buckfastleigh, in 2007.

Cover image: detail from *Some Rain, Slapton Ley Series VII, 2005* (charcoal on arches paper, 66 x 104 cm) by Sarah Gillespie. Reproduced from *The Slapton Ley Project* (White Lane Press, Plymouth, 2007) by permission of the artist. Copyright © Sarah Gillespie, 2007.

table of contents

book one	in the fields of megiddo	7–39
book two	at the stones of pure marble	41–47
book three	the waters of bitterness	49–103
book four	at the gates of paradise	105–112
afterwords		115–121
notes to the text		123–141
bibliographical sources		142–144
acknowledgements		145

[Hillel] also used to say: If I am not for myself, who is for me, But if I am for my own self [only], what am I, And if not now, when?

[BT Aboth 1;14 (8)]

book one

in the fields of megiddo

And the king of Babylon smote them, and put them to death at Riblah in the land of Hamath. So Judah was carried away captive out of his land.

[2 Kings 25:21]

I

    imploded
            warriors
                    stroma

     as hillel the elder   watched a skull
       float upon the face of the water

         sewers opened
         flow of raw art

vessels cracked banks   rats crawled ashore

        implex of reason
    sprung from *eagle of córdoba* s
      stain enlightened sky

   scourge of tongue   broken star
     gravelled words
      refracted light
    as
   sacred scrolls
cradled mountains cities   oceans

it were as if a dance
    of two companies
cratered monochrome image over hebron

     lugworm
     leucoma
     lenticular lesion

 for sound   lies in rhythms   speech

last man orders from ship-soiled sailors arrived on shore

        blood from the book
        blood from the tongue

    fent   figments of flesh
        erased their wounds
as   daemon death dipped
    reed-quivered fingers
into cold metallic alphabets

& gouged gods writ into
    grift appointed universe

      listen to the wandering ear
    far greater than maimonides eye
for *shimon bar kokhbah*
has stepped out of jacob s covetous stall

  man of destiny
anointed
    your
      glory
        lies
beneath   white wippen waters star-studied earth

  as the angel   of
      history
skims deceitful brooks rivers that fail

II

broke this   this spell   this
  conatus of desire
    dissolved

    brocard pretensions
    of *brocatelle* dreams

        this god of   love
          is
          not
          this
          god of love

        but another s love
        like love
        from love
        over-flows

        so
abide not in   love
    but be
      in
        love

not this love of singular reason

    with its
multiplicities of shapes
      figures
  &&
identities
    of shadows

      nor this love
  trapped in ironic gaps of reason
with its cunning intellects   of resplendent logic   denied

      &&
    become not an other self
    wrapped in loves attributes
      with her parables
        sheathed
  in orichalceous
      mountains of gold

        that other self
as pale as silver tried in a crucible seven times

     like the self
that spins its webs through inextricable
            distances of   time
    with love fashioned
        from in-dwellings of love
          abandoned
               or
inflected through an interstitial
       difference of sound
    with its lustres of grace
trapped between the visible and indivisible
   against the sheaf of a tongue
      or
     the pearl
         of a tear

III

1

from   beginning   to beginnings
  from before   the   beginning
    god boiled beelzebub in fire

the god that squashed the fly
  that basked in ineffable suns
the god that severed the heads
    of seven dead rabbits
   the gods from gods
old ghost   company

gods ghoul-stricken strangled
    cumulate clown

           rats tails twitching
whenever death disturbed the narrow streets of luz

2

      standing alone in the garden
      dressed in an old grey-green coat
      regimental tie / regulation cloak

    remembered
how last admirable legion
    late hyacinth
strewn against jacob s winter bloom

could not remember
    laburnum
    how leaves
  tress   of   trees
sycamores turned into   stone

    forgot
they plucked violas from snow
 whenever they scattered death in the larch
   or planted misery
      under cedars of lebanon

3

    balsam oil for libation
    sistrum charters
    chalcidian soothsayers
    scanners
    cutters of heavens
      & star-gazers

but regulus redoubled his endeavours
    suckled blood

  from the rod of their mouth
  & the breath of their lips

 sung accordion scented sounds
   catacoustics for the soul

   children s screaming-&-wailing
  their infant voices immured inside the city walls

what then shall i answer when i am reproved
egyptian / chaldean / syrian / babylonian / roman / german

    forged iron tongues
   hammered from spikenard words
    bent on diasporas gravid anvils
   as measured in alphabets of ginger
    peeled from the floor

  death-masques carved in invincible clay

  this were the knowledge what tampered

4

 impassioned
 tear-drop melted her eye
 when
 she told me
 of tigers
 slaughtered
 teeth of wild beasts
 used against charms

  then inveigled me
   with derision
  like a ladle
   turning gruel

       that old semitic race
       flavoured with money
   stewed in corruptions of dreams

5

  mice faroed
    by cargo
      & wheel

    hand cut/ scourge
four-score
    wound
       jewel-scarred face
slit lip/
   snarled grin

whipped mongrel / gypsy / serb /   hebrew or jew

    death-rattle
harrowed jacob s slattern star

    split
  the seven sacred numbers
  soaked in rubicon red

6

labour of cottars
gramary
language of first fruit covered with fig
      glazed ice /
    cracklured-eye /
    lear
   lustres of gloze
  grizzled seed-pod
trodden   / sand sprinkled under foot

7

    rent words wrenched from wars

      severed limbs
        glistened
      songs drunken
    danced distance deliverance

      let us sing his praise
    from our honeyed tongues
     migrating on iron wings
sprung from manichean machines ruthless eloquence

8

  does abraham still lie in the arms of sarah
  and you reciting those predicant prayers
      of incipient blessings
    stitched through salutary nets
       of salvation

  listen to the five
patriarchs buried
       under
       stone
    still sleeping

9

i have dreamed   i have dreamed

    from *al-andalus*
  to dreams not yet lived

almond   birch thistle
    shevelled songs of the thrush

       first that familial smell of the crowd
        then that near distant scent of fear
         carried on the hiss of hatred
that lies beyond the range of ordinary hearing
  then
the chill wind / & crackling of walls
    that heralds the howling and ruthless mob

        mesmeric / penumbras
          acrid smoke
        burnt limbs / oiled
         like greek acrobats
     their flesh slued through mourning

croup & saw dust clung to the martyrs lungs

IV

1

  the man in the grey-green overcoat
  lent me an old newspaper umbrella
i still remember how it folded outwards

                   we studied
crude diagrams of northern constellations
their spectral motors linked us to earth

  we
    learnt
how the wings of a bat
  quivered the green porcelain sky

eloquent theories
  stuttered out of
    old romantic tales

      drift wood
      / lagan /
  consonants
  crushed on
    slaggèd shore

      2

all
through that night
sat near
by my father
remembered him
bridling tears
riding
palomino steeds of regret

brattling fear-bucking
stallions bronco-backed dreams

still craving
ambitions empty
sacks of greed

all
through that night
sat near
by my father
coveted
him
in coverts of pride

marot elohim /
    (visions of god)
  like
    ezekiel
      waiting for a kiss

3

        in a corner
        of a room
my father s dreams still fit in ruins

           remnants of compassion s gentle touch
      first carried me
        then succoured me
        at arm s length
suffered me derisions
        as he ground down my bones
           into dust

        dis-infected
       soiled sheets cleft
    to that imprint of nothing
        to which
i have grown accustomed

4

once upon a time i stepped into a dream that drew me inexplicably towards a circuitous passage leading inevitably to an impassable street near by an old wooden gate built into a wall surrounding a garden overgrown with a single *briar-rose* draining the purling well of sound

          dark semblance of my mother tongue
            curdled
     around
         familiar drone
           of threshing machines
         dampened
            patch /
               inter-leaved

V

  those irascible gifts not given
   love stolen from the fifteen souls
     drowning in the narrow street
  this was the singular not the particular
    neither the one nor the fifty-nine

   watchman what of the night

    so
   the seven sons of ishmael
    carried their burden abroad

this was the wisdom of ice the light of fire
 & the sound of the horn
   still not heard in *jabneh*

 each dawn
   wakens another memory
just as that memory weakens its memory

  but
if the morning cometh then so does the night

    i will set me a lamp at my feet
    & wait
  in the absence of your glory
   & sit
  in the shadow
   of your inalienable allegory
   that indivisible other of the self

i will stand me upon my watch and set me upon the tower

    here lies
   the eternal stutterer of laws

       the donary of imponderable dowers
       the
  squanderer
                of irrefragable alms

let not your faith be cast on the rip of a dice
nor the glance of an eye   measured in dendrons
              of silence

  then a voice
        shone forth
            &   i saw it call

  write the vision and make it plain upon tables
     that a man may read it swiftly

    but if the vision should tarry
  wait for it   for it will surely come

then god closed the abyss and sealed it with his name

    yesterday his voice will be torn from the book
tomorrow his face was erased from the dead
      & soon this   love poem
  like
this love poem   could not be read /
   without reference to infinity

VI

1

    bright
    white word
   woven
   through the needle of an eye

    the   silent and audible voice
        circulating the ocean

like the moaning of doves
    tabouring upon her breast
      that tarnished leaf s
extrinsic order of encumbered grace

          zion
     ploughed as a field
    her benedictions
     dismembered

her leavened-love   forgot

    the way
 they blackened pomegranate seeds
whenever they scattered the earth with pogroms

what aileth thee now

  watch   the watcher
sward in sun-encased camphor
   all curdled
under babels barbed-wired walls

        2

when *judah ben baba* measured out grief
   between usha and shefara'm

  he forged faith
  with
tear-drops of love
      spread from
      those iron
  spear-heads of death

        egregious harm
           litotes
                raggèd
           moon
        doused
              in fetid waters

              3

     bright white spot on the hand
          turned white
       blemish on the upper lip
     blemish on the white of the eye

        shadow of shadows

    scourge of swords
    whetted by words
& blooded in the ten places of banishment

        ceresin
    puckered love from fire
      before flavour
      departed the fruit

              4

   mist of dew-drop
    hearts whirret
        reflux of
     souls   magnified

cracked/ lambent lament
    sprung from impotent earth

        menagerie of fools
      convex of littoral dreams

        lamprey of clam
     cut from ranzeled stone

  all for the love of god
     buried under ruin

5

    desire   form
      brought/ fluvial
from   beyond
  taught
    impotent space
       divined

leeched cruor love spirit & soul

      necrotic   silhouette
black lantern s shadow   nescient   pearl

    death mask of   jew / scent lilac
     lost   amethyst
       casket of
     leaves
        tress of love
      burnished by clay
      five loaves
    fired from twisted snakes
  fertilised in the ovens of a*kh*nai

6

  the single most important piece of evidence
    that i possess is this silken clew
of ruddled yarn this speckled thread
  of stencilled shroud this fettled cloth
    of surplice draped around a throne

7

    purple wave / brittle sea
       pearlite psalm / sprung from   rutilant joy

  our vestments robbed the life-majestic snare
            the golden tower
      a thousand pearl of peacock eye

8

    though your sins be crimson
      or as red as dyed wool
i will turn them whiter than snow
      whiter than the fleece
        of the new-born lamb

  knock this nail into that holy place

      && then let your heart
make a keeping to my keeping/ a protection to my protection
      but do not sever the golden leaf
        from its marbled shawl

    withered clouds of sempiternal earth
    the voice that sings in the window

      the shadows of leaves
  glistening on murmuring waters

        wild goats rutting
           crenulate mantra
        canticles of song

then the king of babylon smote them
  and put them to death at riblah
      in the land of hamath

dweller on the frontier
does your voice still carry
from beyond the echo

&

does the assiduous student at *jabneh*
still protect his orchard   all around

9

engravings of the signet
revealed
the faith still hidden

hieroglyphs   scratched
snow-blackened ice

spliced stones
obedience
from orphaned tongues

10

it was ·
as if the breath of a sigh
could quiver only a half / of her body

so they cut off the branch & threw it into the fire
so   they cut off the branch & threw it into the fire
     so   they cut off   the branch   &   threw it into the fire

ash threaded through cyprus cedar & lime

veiled
 coefficient of death
   calculating
                              for example

proskurov　　odessa　　　toledo　　　　barcelona
　　　　　tur malka
　　　　　　　　　　bethar

　　　　　　　may be even
　　　　　　　　　　　　　　　belsen

　　let bright scarlet tinctures　　flower
　　　　　　　　　from
　　　gehinnoms blackest flame
when deaths ensnare their vessel of finest gold

　　these enclitic memories shaped like crowns
　　　　ploughed into the fields of megiddo

VII

1

　　　from moment to moment
　　　　　speaks this tongue
　　　its cunning ruse of reason

　　　　　　　sorrows
　　　　　　　　　　clipped　　　lilacs
　　　　luck transects sunbeams
　　　　　　　　tapped pools of samphire

　　csárdás book　　of　　hours

　　forsworn are the rods of the word

　　but he blessed the comet as it flew through orion
　　　　for it had broken the spell
　　　　　　that bound him to the
　　　　　　　　seventh firmament

        glottis   scattered
          lights   divined
            purple vellum flower
         as fear
marked music in the manifest

2

howl cypresses
for cedars have fallen
      howl you oaks of bashan
      for the stately forest is laid low

where then are the protean intellects
      who crave   impenetrable forests

     ravaged
  wits warm earths violets
    strewn scammony
    shimmering
dark maelstroms
    from embittered wine

those   premonstrant protocols of sleep

    your
    pulsar tears
   quivered
songs encyclical silence
salvaged five parts of the soul

3

     then raba reasoned thus
belshazar calculated and made a mistake
  i have calculated and made no mistake

4

      the three keepers of the door
      the academy of the sky

        the gates of weeping
    the veil that was rent /   the shroud that was torn

     the earth becomes like a pillow rolled up tight

  fragments of ink
  turned milk into fire

desipient dust spread from the evil tongue

    baculine blood spat
        inside the line of the law

    the stone
    that stained their faith

here is the thorn
    that lies in the heart of the fig

  make ready the buckler and shield
    then sound the timbrel & blow the horn

  for
shimon bar kokhbah
    has twisted
    the crimson-white
      braids
        that bind
          the hands
        from
          the fingers
            he severed

5

    let us grind the last sheaves of wheat
       gleaned from the last gleanings
          of this   the last harvest

    let us sing the sweet harp and the psaltry
      for   wine
         summer fruits and oil
          are already gathered in our vessels

    then let us sip from the well of palm-trees
    lest we forget to speak
      in the speech of palm-trees

            then let our hearts
           skim this poem s
           enamelled imagination

for rebellion s already built into bethar s sacred soil
& her last harvests are ploughed into her city walls

  late autumn meadows
      augur scallion-figures of death
  with their daggers
        plunged into
    imminent futures

6

    what if the shell protend the kernel
  what if the righteous bow down
    before the yoke

then the lord said unto job
      the waters are congealed like stone
          and the face of the deep is frozen

canst thou bind the chains of the *pleiades*
or loose the threads of orion

7

she walked silently through his sleep
halted near the twisted fork in the road
stooped down low
plucked out truth stuck in the cricoid of his throat

mute love / cleaved love
stuttered   loves
luxury of smiles

VIII

1

anointed visions
of inordinate war
bushidos of love
consumed in fire

ethmoid
tongues
encloistered words
sprung
from the spite of
the curse that was causeless

contumacious desire
ordained /
zealous pride
contraplex scourged
encaustic   lips   of bellicose rank
now engendered from god s velocity

      then in bethar
for three and a half years
                      elazar sat in sackcloth and ashes
         until one day
a samaritan entered the city by means of a drain
      &   feigned speak with elazar

      and when that samaritan was taken to *kokhbah*
        he infected this fear into kozibas ear

your uncle trades death with your enemies

   whereupon   koziba
      gladly
trampled his uncle elazar
            to death

                2

     pulse of insanity
riddled inside the city of refuge

   swallows swooped
              into the bottomless abyss
 or
perched on the rim
     of the shadow of its ridge
as hope ebbed slowly from the edge

  it was
not the first golden candlestick
    that poisoned his lip
but the curse of the sage
    that cleaved
  night
    from
      its day

3

rabbi jose said
    twilight is like   the twinkling of an eye

like the blue flaxen thread turned white

    like the white flaxen thread
    they tied to the parchment skin

    or like the precept of fringes
but not for the one who digs a niche in his own grave

    the clue within a clue
    like the prescribed limit
that oblates sorrow from each generation

    moonlight sparkled sunlight
      daggers twisted through
   the plaited wreaths of her golden hair
    as god measured out vengeance
    according to the old viaticums

IX

1

    refracted
  light
enucleated light
    as zions vineyards
      ploughed into earth
time s future crimes
    eradicate
    the ten martyrs
similitudes of death

        doves wings
            carried
                carrion
            from the ruins of gaza

so
they put out his eyes and carried him to babylon

let them
fashion
love
from
madder
similor
or vermilion

such strange familiars concealed under sylvan veils

    he said
        i am your sign
    but
the five silenced voices
    hovered over him
        when sacramental flames
        burnished the superfluous

    say
the days are at hand and the word of every vision

2

    it was said that on this day
    the tables of the law were shattered
        apostomos burned the scroll of the law
        &
    an idol was placed
      in the temple

it was said that on this day
they bound all the children inside the scrolls of the law
then burnt them in fire

it was said that on this day
they wrapped each of her seven sons
into his own prayer shawl
then buried them under perlite and gold

it was said that on this day
bethar was captured
and the city of jerusalem
ploughed up

this was the reflux of time
that split the memorial stone

  & this was the trap with no corn

3

verdant waters
ripened by the blood that seeps
from the caverns of paneas

like the blood that flows into the great sea
or the blood that flowers from the twelve-folded springs
that irrigate our dreams

like the blood that dislocates language
whenever words refuse to bleed

so they inscribed the name on a shard
&
cast it into the deep

our bones are dried up and our hope is lost

so
he
sealed
gods
secret-name
inside
the sanctum
concealed behind the sepulchre
of the holy letter

then he placed the letter
inside a vessel of papyrus

then he floated
the vessel of papyrus
onto the oceans of bitterness
& prayed that the sacred name
might be blotted out
in its waters

this is the wheel that spins through heavenly wheels
&
this is the wheel that never stops turning

4

what if the pious man should sit in the shadow of god
&
watch as his voice ripples upon water

fragments of faith
that cannot taste the thirteen names
that glistened
on boaz s arrant breath

a thousand year solitude
cradled gazelle schulammite & / the red rose of sharon

X

      beyond the azimuth
         through the secret garden
to the palisade where a *fleur-de-lis*
             leads to another road

    light of azoth
      flected flecks
            from her golden hair

  segholate petals float
     on pellucid light
       split brittle
        fluorescent moonlight
days lengthening
            loves masquerade
deaths dappled shadows shimmering over
       cedar cypress & mimosa

XI

1

blood spread through the narrow streets
   whenever carcasses were hung out to dry

         the sallow hand out-reached
  the white pitched sky
      &
vaulted tent

  so
he drew a cordon
      around
          the landscape

                    then
        in coniine anger
                    he cut down
                    the conifers that built his house

    obtund brittle bones
        abandoned diaphanous phantom flesh
                dissimulated chrysalis

        lancinate / laniary

        for drunken retribution
            were the songs they sang

                        2

if she be a wall we will build upon it a silver battlement
if she be a door we will panel it in cedar

                        3

            dare not   linger in the garden
    for my lover is listening   to your every breath

            & do not let me hear your voice
            lest i forget
            the sea castles rolling
                around
the citadels of shushan

                        4

    lilith s daughters dug deep into rotund flesh
                her virgin lovers
            turned arrows into sand
        fettled laughters
                wrought

    pleasures writ   erased
   numbers
      catalogue s

          cain s voice   echoed
                from fossil stone

5

garth dampened earth   dug covens cosmogony of glass

  cobbled tongue/ splinter'd bone/ stuttered note
    fabled breeze / split / faburdened cloth
    faith succumbed to acquiescent death

6

    oh my once
  beautiful and demanding hellenism
let me drink deep draughts
      from your evil waters
   so that i might hear
    once again
  the cynic martyrs song
   whisper cholers
      virulent rancoured ire

7

come near so that you might hear
  how the slave pierced
    this golden newel through
       his master s ear

  broken odes /
  garnered epithalamions
   from demons ruins

death rattled
vellum roughened star

    but
his hearts-ventricles snapped abruptly
      when his enucleated eyes
    pierced futures diminished sight

     the sallow hand
      the lode-star tear
      the graceful kiss
     a crust of bread

  life forsaken for the warmth of skins
the caress that shrouds the many coloured coats

8

then they slew them at riblah
  & the captain of the guard
    burnt the house of the lord
      and the king s house
        and all the houses of jerusalem
          even
every great man s house burnt he with fire

so the sons of zedekiah moved northward
    traversing the lower road
      dogs tethered to their wrists
        blistered marks of steel
     masked jaws of death snapped shut

Our Rabbis taught:
Four men entered the
'Garden', namely Ben
'Azzai and Ben Zoma,
Aher, and R[abbi]
Akiba. R. Akiba said
to them: When y[ou]
arrive at the stones of
pure marble say not,
Water, water. For it is
said: He that speaketh
falsehood shall not
be established before
mine eyes. Ben 'Azzai
cast a look and died.
Of him Scripture says:
Precious in the sight
of the Lord is the
death of His saints.
Ben Zoma looked and
became demented.
Of him Scripture
says: Hast thou found
honey? Eat so much as
is sufficient for thee,
lest thou be filled
therewith, and vomit
it. Aher mutilated
the shoots. R. Akiba
departed unhurt.

[BT Hagigah 14b (90–91)]

book two

at the stones of pure marble

And God made the firmament, and divided
the waters which were under the firmament
from the waters which were above the
firmament; and it was so.

[Genesis 1:7]

XII

Simeon ben Azzai

i have a tradition from the mouth of the seventy-two elders

    that my hectic love
  still flowers in the hedonic gardens at tiberias

    but alas
    my hesitation
can not testify from these unclean lips

   nor count the ban against
the drum that atones for my sins

your absence like the dove departed
    was a sacrifice magnified seven-times

but still my silence
    can not satisfy all doubt
        when even the slightest doubt
           would have rendered it invalid

this opaque glass hung from the myrtle tree
    is like the one who erred

    but
  true to his principles
this assiduous student sleeps

    and in his dreams
digs at the loose cimolion earth
   so that he might plant a corner of his fear
in that intimate space
    that stands
  between the proximity of two worlds

    let him write upon writing
so that he might divide the one from the other

    & let me cut his unclean lip
    before burning my tongue with its bruise

    lest he whisper his love
        to that darkening ring
    as it spreads around her nipple

Simeon ben Zoma

  who
can cultivate such fragrant words
    or temper the bitterness
        that drips from his trembling lips

    here is
the sin offering
    &
here is the burnt offering

        &
here is the knife that twists in the cell of the leper
like the life that no longer shoots forth as an arrow

    let him abide outside of the temple
      so that he might sleep
        under the yellow-white shadows
      cast by the waves of the sea

    & let him sit at the gates of weeping
    like the eagle   that   hovers on water
      her beaks
    secreting
    liquid myrrh

     for he must reap
    what cannot be sown
 and then gather together all the blank spaces
      that lie above
       below
 in the beginning
               at the end
       and

in between the   sections and the columns

   let him sing whatever is written in flesh
    for his preachers gullet is still not empty

    but beware the song
   for his soft honeyed tongue
  might still break the bones of god

      Elisha ben Abuyah [Aher]

   affiliate zealot
 proselyte twists in twisted zealous zeal

    still searching
   the thirteen souls
  that meditate upon idolatry

  let that remnant echo
    echo
from the other s daughters son

so what if the curtain behind the veil
   should reveal a window in the sky
  when all those silken tongues
   that burnished pearls
     now lick the dust

      a catapult of bones
        concealed in palinodes
      churned about
              his mouth

      let him grasp
        the vessel of broken glass
    so that he might drink from the book
        as the black words burn
    & the white letters fly from the fire

        but do not knock
      on his empty martyrs nest
        lest you forget to infuse
frankincense with columbine & myrtle

          Rabbi Akiba

when we lay in the house of concealment
you refused to cast the straw from my hair
you were my learning   my silver cord
my golden bowl   my pitcher by the fountain
      my wheel in the cistern

    but who was the weaver who knotted your thread
                        &
  who was the preacher who kneaded your dough

        men of arm and men of tongue
          you have planted your silence
            in this lozenge of saffron

          still the retrospective man
        can not sit in the lap of the gods

    so pluck up your trees and be gone

            we scattered
        incense balm and embers
    over oceans that have no visible ends

       we walked through bitter-sweet rivers
         to the margent halls of hewn stone
            saw seven forms inner voice
                 pierce the abyss

         but
    i blotted it out
    when i planted
the ten saplings of redundant speech

                    &
                   now
             i cannot forget
          the bright white blemish
              white like snow
         white like the lime on the wall

         white like the skin of an egg
          white like the coat of a lamb

           that beautiful white blemish
         white like wine mingled with snow

       but your counsel of serpents revealed
       only five fragments from the broken stool
                      &
                the three worlds
              that i never profaned

                      &
            the curve of your lip
       was as gentle as the reed   engraved
              in the fields of   white

and the sound of your voice was as soft as the dust
scattered under the soles of my feet

so i looked into the eye of the serpent
& learnt how to walk through its needle of thorns

& i glanced into souls rhythms speech
& saw how to burnish the embers
so that they might burst through its fruit

& then
i poured water into the mouth of my teachers
for their worms   like threads of tradition
fenced me around

where then are the tithes that i buried
under the old wooden gate by my grave

& where are the stripes of my flesh
that the romans laid out
on their market-stalls

Our Rabbis taught: How does one dance before the bride? Beth Shammai say: The bride as she is. And Beth Hillel say: Beautiful and graceful bride'!

[BT Kethuboth 16b–17a (92)]

book three

the waters of bitterness

Woe to the bloody city!
It is all full of lies and rapine

[Nahum 3:1]

XIII

1

    curled white skin
  carved
      curved willow pen
     cold metallic ink

     spliced hallowed bones
   severed one from another

     scraped curette flesh
   from the un-kempt dead

2

    wisdom has built her house
     hewn her seven pillars
  prepared the feast   mixed the wine
        set the table

now come near
  and hear
    how the blank spaces
                  above
                  and below
    between the sections
       &
    the columns

at the beginning
                &
                        at the end of the scroll

    defile the hand

3

       black fire
  forged   from invisible filigrees
      formed   fugitive affectations
     fount
  of erotemic veils

  sliced
   the   eighty-five   infinite
inviolable impossibilities

     burnt seven crowns
       from
   the twelve indelible spheres

encompassed   circensian squared circles
scattered soil over seeds sacred dominion

  those cruel instruments of jacobs ladder
       reached
        for
   dark *edaphic* souls

4

           exiled
  to the alien lands shrouded
in the deep shadow of the buzzing of wings

  vineyards fertilised
    by pure-plumed blood
      sprung from verdant pastures

fountains of living water
      dis/in/tered / izzat tongue

5

    when they camped at *refidim* there was no water to drink
    so moses struck the rod of god on the rock of horeb
        and water issued forth

    we have a teaching in accord with *resh lakish*
        that moses went up in a cloud
        was covered by the cloud
        and was sanctified by the cloud
    in order that he might receive the *torah* for israel

    now they hew
        broken cisterns that hold   no water

6

    he has put his name within me
    metatron in gematria the almighty

silenced crewel flagellant divisions
    depleted/ paronyms / cadence /

seal up   their walls of flesh and bones
    so that no evil word nor sound   / can issue forth
from their tongues   nor breath range over earth

7

    if a man in a fit of jealousy
    believes his wife has deceived him

    he shall bring her to the priest
    together with an offering of barley flour
    this is the meal offering of jealousy
    the meal offering of remembrance
    that recalls wrongdoing

    then the priest shall take earth from the floor of the tabernacle
        and place it in an earthen-vessel of sacral water
            this is the water of bitterness
    that will induce the spell
    in the woman who has gone astray in defilement

            then the priest shall administer
        the curse of adjuration   to the woman
                      &
        having administered the curse
        he shall put it down in writing
    then   rub it off   into the water of bitterness

            then the priest
must make the woman drink the water of bitterness
            that induces the spell
        so that the spell-inducing water
            may enter into her
            and bring on bitterness
                      &
        her belly shall distend
        and her thigh shall sag
    and the woman shall become a curse
            among her people

but if the woman has not defiled herself
                              and is pure
        she shall be unharmed
        and able to retain her seed

            8

        here lies
        the falsehood
        of blank pages

let the scribe write it in dust

                words
             like silken veins
                threaded through
          lattice-leaves / fire-flowered / laughter

      let the scribe engrave the scars
           described in her flesh

   waves   weaves deaths   ruins
         deprecated   dreams

           silence
            spun
              from
        the noise of grindstones
                & the
        eighty thousand battle trumpets
            still assembled at *bethar*

       vibrations too
          distant to
                        break love s
         dis/harmony s distant crescendo

            psalms
              inflections
                snapped
                   like lilacs flying
                        from the grave

                    9

       hear this o priests/ attend o house of israel
             give ear o royal house
        for right conduct is your responsibility/
          but you have been a snare to mizpah
           and a net spread out over tabor

10

crafted creosote
from epicureans crescent credence tables
like that creance
twisted around the spartoi tooth
pulled from the serpents jaw

cresset soliloquies silenced
sordid metaphysical s existence

let him extract
the thorn that lies inside
the maturity that already belongs to the fruit

11

let him light the golden lamp
or mount the libyan ass
or read the words
written on the tables of my heart

but what   of those holy books that may not be read
&
what   of those sacred writings
that may not be saved from the fire

let him crave   what he never yearned
but dared not cover his nakedness
with the cochlea that failed

12

larynx arraigned
torn scripts from *akibas* flesh
hearts engraved
minds deranged

   sonant walls of jerico
    broken
by the last blast of the horn

  glottis / throat / palate / lips / teeth/   tongue

  the intellect has become
like a flock of eagles caught   in the beak of a dove

     13

rabbi joshua ben levi stated that *gehenna* has seven names
the nether world   destruction   pit   tumultuous pit
 miry clay   shadow of death   and   underworld

resh lakish said
  if paradise is in the land of israel
    then its gate is *beth shean*
  if it is in arabia   its gate is *beth gerem*
   and if it is between the rivers
     then its gate is
        dumaskanin

     14

  so what if they cast   metaphors in matters
    of sleep
  or ponder
imponderable solutions
  such as   could god ever covet
the hatred that satan implanted in his neighbours heart

 implausible
  but not implacable
because their brunonian bleached bones
  were already susceptible to
 the trans-magnetic flow of ions

15

      flesh & transcriptions of   flesh
        skin & sinews of skin

   veins   drowning in vessels of blood

  cruor drawn from love engorged
    on quotidian principles of time

        those
    dark sayings of the harp
      from the ones who plundered

16

    then the officers of the troop in the open country
& their men with them heard that the king of babylon
had put gedaliah   son of ahikam   in charge of the region
  so that he might reign over those men women and children
of the poorest land who had not been exiled to babylon

    then johanan the son of kareah
and all the officers of the troops that were in the field
  came to gedaliah   in mizpah   and said to him
do you know that king baalis of ammon   has sent
    ishmael son of nethaniah   to kill you
      but gedaliah did not believe them

17

    let me say only this
  that the putrefaction that swells
    from the thules of oblivion
      can no longer ensnare
      the poet s desire
to seek out   the feasts of crematoriums

                    nor
                  drink
         from the sacred fountains of
            their grid-rigid memories

               gifts amputations
                 woven through
                grief-frozen-tears

         for revenge lay fallow
            before god
                        ever rooted
                  his foot in the soil

         now let the eagle of córdoba
         call forth the sound of *our* blood

                          18

    then johanan   the son of kareah   spoke secretly   to
        gedaliah in mizpah   let me go and strike down
          ishmael son of nethaniah   before anyone knows about it
    for otherwise he will kill you   and all the judeans
          gathered about you will be scattered
            and the remnant of judah will perish

    but   gedaliah son of ahikam   said to johanan son of kareah
    do not touch ishmael   for you speak falsely against him

                          19

         execution by the sword was performed thus
         the condemned man was decapitated by the sword
         as is done by the civil authorities

                    rabbi judah said
                    this is a hideous disfigurement

      but his head was laid on a block
              and severed with an axe

        they replied
        no death is more disfiguring

once the grandfather of rabbi peridas
found a skull lying near the gates of jerusalem
      and upon it was written
        this and yet another
it was said that this was the skull of *jehoaikim*

        once at kefer saba
    they found a skull stuck in the root of a sycamore tree

              20

    clerical spheres of incompetence
        projective conscriptions
        of presumptive grace

      those secret words not yet spoken
    burnt babels skeletal bones
        scattered
       the five haggard vowels
  hung upon consonant babylonian walls

      warnings en-snared in nets of imagination
  hieroglyphs   eclipsed   the infinite

      transgressors of the temporal plane
      trespass
     threnody
    elegies
  of mundane memories
 forgot
those circuitous paths woven around

21

            then in the seventh month
      ishmael son of nethaniah son of elishama
who was of royal descent & one of the kings commanders
        came with ten men to   gedaliah   son of ahikam
           and they ate together at mizpah

    then ishmael   and the ten men who were with him
arose / struck down gedaliah with the sword & killed him
              all because the king of babylon
        had put gedaliah in charge of the land

        then ishmael killed all the judeans
         who were with gedaliah in mizpah
   and all the chaldean soldiers stationed there

22

    removed
   damaged lagan
spilt bone / scarious flesh / buried by sand

     the deaf & the drowned
 drifting from sea-shore to sea-shore
       as ocellate waves
 circumnavigate the circumference
    around the meniscus universe

    euclidean oracles
out-stretched   beyond   the lineate calculus

  &   what if all those torn-out tongues
    could cultivate their licit speech
      in those illicit margins
    gouged out of god s
          myriad stars

23

      nahum the scribe said   i have a tradition from
rabbi me'asha   who received it from abba   who received it
from the *zugoth*   who received it from the prophets
        as an *halachah* of moses from sinai
     that a man who sows his field with two kinds of wheat
       and makes it up into one threshing-floor
must give one pe'ah   if two threshing-floors two pe'ahs

24

    translucent light
      embraced
    the sordid light

the humming birds
   mocking harmony

the rays of a thousand suns
    shone upon decadent earth

flesh
  out-stretched
    light
      cast
    from
     cracked   cartesian skulls
delicate shells   of mercators obverse fold

25

  now the cistern into which ishmael cast all the dead bodies
  of those men whom he had slain   in the affair of gedaliah
was the cistern king asa had constructed on account of his fear
     of king baasa of israel
  that was the cistern which ishmael filled with corpses

XIV

1

seven white mules
    trampled the allegorical
the three hundred and sixty five by-ways
      penitent
          periegesis
              masquerading   as death

    the minds metaphors twist in aliquant delight

do not   let the contentious woman   pacify your anger
      as aarons doubts once quenched our flame

    for our mutual friend phinehas
    can not speak about satan
without drinking   those sacral waters
      infused with sand

2

and behold six men came from the way of the upper gate
    which lieth towards the north
every man with his slaughter weapon in his hand
and one man in the midst of them clothed in linen
    with a writers inkhorn by his side

3

intaglio / infidels
    rigor
      of
accursèd intellect
bamoth
riven by acicular desire

      discourse dignified   theology acidified

          chambers of the soul
          hearts redaction

     integers of   alien propositions
              &
       palladian amplifications
   concealed inside gematrian symmetry

       arks of the rainbow
refracted oceans secret votive seed of flowers
         offered gifts of love
as martyrdoms rained down upon palladium earth

4

                and the lord called to the man
  clothed in linen with the writers inkhorn at his side
    and said to him   pass through the city of jerusalem
and put a mark on the foreheads of the men
      who moan and groan because of all the abominations
    that are committed in it   to the others   he said
    follow him through the city
and strike   show no pity or compassion   kill off
  greybeard   youth   and maiden   women and children
   but do not touch any person who bears the mark

5

forged
          footsteps
                    echo
                              echo

     celandine for memory / memory for memory
    clandestine memory stripped from counterfeit memory

```
        memories of memory lost in resuscitated sleep
     memory
             of blessèd memory
         memories stolen from memories
                  memories stacked upon memories
              built
        upon
     a universe of shadows
                & shoahs
 emanating from emaciated earth
```

                                6

```
      fidelity of faith
         grants them the right to dig their own graves

   remember     to remember           always to remember
          that the prima facie    precept
  is to remember        & remember    to remember
              & to witness the witness
              & to search through the ashes
           so as to   excavate all traces that accumulate

         &          having remembered
             to remember
      to remember not to forget
         to become the traitor to memory
     so
              that you
   might    learn how to integrate     those memories
```

                                7

```
       then from the roof-top   bands of young priests  threw
            the keys of the temple      high   into the sky
  &      as the keys flew heavenwards   the priests
                     jumped headlong into the fire
```

this was the day of perplexity
with kir shouting and shoa at the mount

i see only two
but i hear the voice of another
it is
the voice of the one who sits amongst the lepers
&
causes the lips of the dead to speak from the grave

8

then the man clothed in linen
with the writers inkhorn at his   side
brought back word saying

i have done as you commanded me

XV

1

he caressed each verse
as if it were   as a precious stone
as a sigh that shattered   only half of her body

& when he set a seal upon the arm
the hand in the temple broke
its clenched fist
held to that singular creed
crimped
from the soul s heart of
hunger

like the fine flour that floats upon the top of the sieve

2

when a certain clod of earth at *beth horon*
was held to be in a presumptive state of uncleanliness
an old man took some sheets soaked in water
and spread them over the earth

after a time some of the earth became moist
then having dug into the moist earth
they found a large pit full of bones

it has been taught
that this was the pit into which ishmael
cast all the dead bodies of the men
whom he had killed *by the hand of gedaliah*

but
surely we should read
by *the affair* of gedaliah not   by *the hand* of gedaliah
for it was ishmael
who slaughtered them at mitzpah

and yet our rabbis have taught
that because gedaliah refused to listen to the advice of johanan
we must   now consider gedaliah as if he too had killed them

but what then of johanan   who did nothing
because he obeyed gedaliah at mitzpah

3

rabbi shila once said
if a man comes to kill you   rise early and kill him first
& having quoted the verse from *torah*
he raised his staff   against the man he believed to be his persecutor
and dashed that man s life blood
against his own garments

4

when four hundred jars of rabbi huna s wine turned sour
rabbi judah went to visit him

the master ought to examine his actions
for should the almighty be suspect of punishing without justice

5

as
the prince of oceans
snapped at their heels
the adulterers ran
like trees felled in a forest
their leaves disintegrating into dust

now let us gather
pharmaceutics and roots from the books of the ancients
so as not to forget
that all our miseries apostasies murders exiles & deaths
in ghettos & diasporas
are still being woven through
zechariah s scrupulousness

6

let him throw a coin into the ocean
so that he does not become
a slave to his pen

then let the children of your children
take refuge under the shadow of his wing

&
let us dance
in the upper-market at sepphoris

      so that we might smell   once again
         the blood of the sin offering
      smeared over the seventy-five staddles
buried under the twenty-eight gateways of knowledge

7

but our dancing soon turned into mourning
      once the king s heart
      turned merry with wine

quick   let his servants pass through our garden
      carrying their contraband
      of gold onyx & juniper

      spoilers
  & spoilers of spoilers
      let us seize the days
of easy money/ flagstones
    pogroms and riots

  dealers   treacherous dealers
traducing greed with the flicker of an eye

8

    the temple of nimrod
  is like a tower that flies in the air

    the broken curtain
like an iron urn / swung in the rhyme

  here is a pouch for your soul
    i have filled it with
    five poisoned arrows
pillaged
  from the quivers of lilith

     the five arrows that once
  pierced your heart with their love

       crushed skull
       of the rose-bud
       shedding its petal

jealousy as cruel as the grave

9

first they riddled his body like a sieve   then left grief
   to watch over him   as flesh withered from its bones

10

    then jeremiah said   to the remnant of judah
  that had escaped death at mizpah
                thus said the lord
be not afraid of the king of babylon   for i am with you
     and will save you   and deliver you from his hand
and i will grant you compassion
    so that the king of babylon
        may also have compassion upon you
  and cause you to return to your own land

  and if you stay in this land i will plant you and build you
     for i repent me
of the evil that i have done unto you

   but all the people   great and small
      and all the captains of the forces
    ignored the words
        of jeremiah
     and fled into egypt
   for they feared
the wrath of the chaldeans

XVI

1

    lest
        nimos the weaver
thread his soft murmuring sound
    through the swirling mists
      that shroud
    the trembling heavens

2

the ten
    the two hundred
      the five thousand & eighty-five
        the six million
     fugitive souls
  the burden of dumah
  whose numbers
haunt
    carnage
wrought
    rivers
        that run thicker than zechariah s   blood
          cut into stone

parchments of flesh
    stitched from death

3

  maimonides memorial tables
    set in   the valley of visions

  far better than babylonian palaces
  sunken under tree-lined roads

4

              god engraved
his   many sacred names
      inside the fathomless well

let them curse the verse that pierced the infinite abyss

         scourge of seven tongues
    wisdom of leaves plucked from fire

5

thus said the lord of hosts   in those days
ten men from nations of every tongue   will take hold
they will take hold of every jew   by a corner of his cloak
and say   let us go with you for we have heard
                                  that god is with you

6

like a hammer that breaks the rock in pieces

the school of rabbi ishmael taught   just as a hammer
is divided into many sparks so every single word that went forth
from the lips of the holy one   blessed be he
     split up into seventy languages

7

          sarcophagus
               cast
      carding / sardonic flowers

wood beams /   / split / cantilevered shawl

     marriage of rainbows

    twisted
       locks / lacklustre smile
     the active intellect of the inner eye
             banquets of love
       circumcised
the dreams   he dared not dream

                8

the words *asher kummetu* indicate blessing
these are the scholars who wrinkle themselves
over the words of *torah* in this world
so that the holy one   blessed be he
shall reveal a secret to them in the world to come
for it is said
       to whom a secret is poured out as a stream

                9

   come   & hear how nebuchadnezzar was alarmed
       for he said to his ministers

did we not cast three men bound into the midst of the fire
   but lo i see four men walking unbound and unharmed
         in the midst of the fire
and the appearance of the fourth is like a son of the gods

              10

   then elijah led *rabbah ben abbuha* into paradise
and said to him   remove your cloak and collect some
  of these leaves   that you may take them with you
    but as rabbah was about to depart   he heard a voice say
   who would so consume his portion of the world to come
      as rabbah has done
whereupon rabbah scattered the leaves
                        and departed

      but since he had carried some of the leaves in his cloak
          it had absorbed some of their fragrance

      so he sold his cloak for twelve thousand denari
      and distributed the money to his sons-in-law

11

     & still
  the heady weight of reason
       can not determine
why the eighty-five names
      could utter   no song

      let us
  hear the sight of her presence
     or
see the voice of her face
    shine through a bright speculum

  but do not sing his praise in the valley of dura
     unless you ask him first
      to smell and to judge
    but not after the sight of his eyes
     nor with the hearing of his ears

    before then do not expect him
  afterwards you may wait for him

    blasted be the bones
of those who would calculate the end

  but let not this secret reproof prevail
    for rabbi torta has already revealed
    how akiba s cheeks sprouted grass
     long after the messiah
             never came

XVII

1

    that it could not be   what   it should not be
        was yet to be done in   its grace
            not   for   nothing
      that full glottal stop   of   the mouth-closed-lung

    intimate
      i
  that smallest letter
    hidden
        between
              lisp & spittle
            split
                indefinite
                  abyss

lost beneath the breath of that infinite being
      the one beyond
    being   the one

that single breath trapped between two indigent letters

      like the love abandoned
  in the quarries of our soul

        floating
  cherry-fold / molten / moulted patina

      hidden
    behind edens   secreted gardens
      with her secret covens
    enclosed
        in heart s mysteries
            perfectly arrayed

    but still he   could n t smell
theleavesthatscentedhiscoat

      another   one
                deluded
  by   ko*kh*ba   the liar/ the star

      and another one
      like all those other
      orphaned sons of gods
that glisten & glide on   rivers that fail

      even
phinehas the favoured one   the prodigal son
was still found wanting/ but not in the encounter

      even in sleep
   could not   efface the deceit
     not one
     but another
       like the one
       that shines in
alampofimpenetrabledarkness

for even akiba the saint
     who danced on water /   intermingled with water
     now sleeps on the lakes
       of   lachesis
  stripped of all consciousness

  just as two beings are joined into one
  the mute becoming of being
the one who was damned   &   the one who was drowned

    wave   altered sound
       &
     blotted it out

daggers that mark impossible places

just as *sh'was*   siglas   signatures   whispered
through asterisks & sigmas
enigmas   metaphors semaphores muzzled
that silence   he yearned for
a language to speak in its saying

2

the barrel   broken
love-wreck shipwrecked at dawn
the fruit of the tree   that never yielded its fruit

a plethora of signs
concealed behind
symbols that spy

nutations of words
spiral around that labyrinthine maze
refuting referents
names
leading
but
nowhere beginning

3

cursed
bloodless corpse
cleansed chasms abyss

daedalus
still limping
chasing the clew
through   importunate sex
his intellect gagged from minotaurs tails   imagined

        the golden arcanum
   vibrating around ariadnian threads
     stolen from mothers weaving
needles of death through their own children s skin

    all the while
the holy one blowing
     his
cunning trumpets of war

4

    pierced   from behind
       seen / but not spoken
   bracketed   close in encounters
priests sprinkled blood /   waters   &   psalters

  baptisms
  caverns
humbled
  by fire

5

could he
  divine
the humming birds white sovereign eye
  its orifice closed in blind originary silence

   like the fathers that carried
   their sons
blanched-bleached-blistered bones
  stenched purpled flesh

   those indelible runes
    seeped
 in soured yellowed-inked-milk

faded flight of foot-print
hovered over
owls
skudler mouth opened

succubous
screeching

6

according to josephus
the entire outer court of the temple
was deluged with the blood
of eighty-five hundred corpses
who now greeted the rising of the sun

XVIII

1

con con contt ttttt   cont / con   tinued
through con son ants
kh-kh-kh-
an*kh*ored aru*kh*
atomised   adjunct

but can the tongues of the dead
still speak in maimonides words
as if all their nonsense could be wrapped
into small sequences
of rabelaisian green gargantuan silences

as if
no other colour could stammer its meaning
even
if set against josef s prepared table

       or trapped between
       his insufferable spittle

peril   of   lov   un-*kh*   un-*kh*

  in spite of this
they dipped their tongues into the inkwell
    && forced the word
       to crawl through the rent
      in the prince s shroud

2

rue goosefoot purslane hill-coriander water parsley
and meadow berries are exempt from tithes
rabbi judah says   aftergrowths of mustard are permitted
rabbi simeon says   all aftergrowths are permitted
but the sages say   all aftergrowths are forbidden

3

    let
his right hand become a fiery law unto them
  not a flacid fist clenched inside his pocket

    the fist that hammers from the left
    the fist that opens from the right

      filamentz of silver forged   from
        figures of adverse gold

    this
      nothing from   nothing
  like
the smell of cumin
        mingled with bread

4

    let the suspicion of blood attach to the stain
      so that the blood of the innocent condemned
         might be hung
  upon the necks of those who witnessed against them

       leaning too
          it / was
only   as if   only is

     cursed be the ones
   who shed the blood of war
      in times of peace
for they too shall be crushed under the building

     but they blew the horn
  & whetted their words at the edge
    their vocal chords honed
 upon   alpha-elements speech-matrix-spirals

zealots   taught black-bleached-black scroll of the law
  torn bacillus   blinded by pains bleary-eyed piston

     stoning & burning
       augured
       anarchy
ordered / anger / misery torments / tortures sufferings
        & deaths

5

     for *rab judah* said in *rabs* name
had but jonathan given david two loaves of bread for his travels
  nob the city of priests would not have been massacred
    doeg the edomite would not have been destroyed
  and saul and his three sons would not have been slain

6

when the children of your bereavement
                          travelled east
they exchanged their coats for swords
            complex oedema

a dream of the vine with three branches
signifies surd wine pressed from those hypocrites hyperboles
  still flavoured with hyssop syrup & thyme

        iniquities
inspired by the counsel of god

  send soldiers to kill him
not cower him into submission

commands   com'   com'   comm' odor of ops

    then joshua said to ulla   in a whisper
   leave silently by the side door
   so that you will not be seen

     but ulla replied
do not make me depart / for my heart is ablaze
        &
our fates shall remain irrevocably entwined

     tread lightly
lest elijah weaken the dawn

7

a rumour was spread
that certain galileans had murdered a man
they came to *rabbi tarfon* and asked him to hide them
the master said   if i do not hide you they will find you

but if i hide you i would be acting contrary
to the statement of the rabbis as to slander
one should not believe it but one should take note of it
                         go you and hide yourselves

8

zealots of war
  our perils lie in your balance

    let the waiting prolong

9

      dredge them here /
drag them against their will

bind them
whip them
scourge them of flesh
safe in
intention
no detail to be spared

blood from the sun
blood from the sac
blood dripping from the sac

this was the story of talos told over & over again
for it was daedalus that carried the corps
in a sac out of athens

 but they caught him / shackled him / hobbled him
hand over foot/ tossed him bound over capitol hill

just like the story of snakes
trapped in the ovens of *aknai*

10

    can the listening ear of redemption
    still hear how the martyrs of lud
    were fed on burnt grass

       & the sins of their charity
       scraped from the dust
       that baladan suckled with pride

11

then moses anger waxed hot and he cast the *tables* out of his hands and broke them beneath the mount and took the calf which they had made and burnt it with fire and ground it to powder and strewed it upon the water
                      and made the children of israel drink of it

XIX

1

    sigh in silence make no mourning for the dead
bind thy headtire upon thee and put thy shoes upon thy feet

2

       the sky pitched leeward
       cedar divided his house
       & the split roots spread
       under the white vaulted tower

    snow-storm a-top   black mountain
       marbled-onyx   sun
  shone upon the corinthian bronze
      of the nicanor gates

       gold   burnished   gold
burette / chalcedony   buhrstone

arms called to arms
as their iron axes shattered on the gates

3

then moses & aaron   nadab & abihu & seventy elders of
israel ascended   and they saw   the god of israel
& under his feet
there was the likeness of a pavement of sapphire
like the very sky for purity
yet he did not raise his hand against the leaders of the israelites
& they beheld god   and they ate and drank

4

terror forced honour   from pride-stained funeral pyres

leprous hands
dissimulating greed
dug into pliant flesh
swords chased in sand
forged aclinic wars
acquiescent deaths

they learnt to shape
the many coloured coat
watch a thousand prisms glisten
as their childrens bodies leavened rivers

5

& he brought out the asherah from the house of the lord
& burnt it at the brook kidron & stamped it small to powder
& cast the powder on the graves of the common people

6

    let them etch their books in blood
    scratch their braggart texts
    with brattled script

    & let their bridled ears
    hear how their servants
    garbled gods-engraved words

7

as for the angel of the covenant that you desire
he is already coming
but who can endure the day of his coming
and who can hold out when he appears
for he is like a smelter s fire and like fuller s lye
he shall act like a smelter and purger of silver
and he shall purify the descendants of levi
and refine them like silver and gold
so that they shall present offerings in righteousness

8

    remember
nebuchadnezzar the scribe became the messenger

    remember
    shebna the scribe
rent what could not be   re-sewn

    remember
how elisha saw it and cried

words whispered from above
words whispered
        from below

    for
you have slain a dead people
 && burned a temple already burned

   wherefore then
are the chariots of israel and the horsemen thereof

9

  so elijah said unto them
take the prophets of baal let not one of them escape
   so they brought them down
  to the brook kishon and slew them there

 this was the double-portion
 & the horror of tongues softly spoken

   thereupon elijah took his mantle and rolling
   it up he struck the water it divided
   to the right and left so the two of
   them crossed over on dry land

 the silent horn snapped
 the sacral vessel opened

11

     first they stood by the conduit
        of the upper pool
   which is in the highway of the fuller s field
     then they marched northwards
       along the lower road
       their legs shackled
    in collars of iron / dogs teeth
      tethered marks wrists
      blistered masks of steel
   masked jaws of death snapped shut

many years later that same road turned east
& ran along stony paths built upon tiny pebbles
quarried from bird-songs bruised memories

      echoed
          lost
              echo

      many years later that same road turned north
              across *velamina* valleys
                  to where white walls
              crushed reeds / covered
                roughened vellum
        coloured lilacs dripped in vitriol

now let your blinded eyes stare into these mysterious pleasures

XX

1

    lode star / stone
synclastic faith crowned
the benedictions that failed

       i / it was
         but
     not as it was

   impotent indifference
cleaving inflections from mountains of zeal

    corrupt   scimitar
cleft life s discordant symmetry

lion / leopard / skink rat raven crow

    love of the chase
   etched into motifs of blood

      2

   what motivated this song
    was that igneous necklace of grace
     my father seeled
      from his mother s
     medallion of tears

      3

when zedekiah rebelled against the king of babylon
nebuchadnezzar moved against him with his whole army
and for two years besieged jerusalem
and built towers against it all around
until the famine had become so acute in the city
that there was no food left for the common people

      4

    let him follow
     the dream
    not
  seek out its interpretation

 let him nest
  inside the secret pockets of my metaphysical vest
 with its dark *coronas*
buried under the rubble of great problems

   but beware
   falling debris
    & flying demons
  just two of the reasons
not to trespass into gabriel s ruined palace

5

        once when rabbi jose
          was travelling on the road
he entered into one of the ruins of jerusalem in order to pray
    elijah   of blessed memory   appeared at the door
        and waited for him to finish
    then *elijah* asked jose   what sound he had heard whilst
    praying inside the ruin   jose replied
i heard a divine voice cooing like a dove and saying

    woe to the children on account of whose sins i destroyed my
        house and burnt my temple   and exiled them among
    the   nations of the world

    but *elijah* replied
  by your life and by your head
      not in this moment alone does it so exclaim
  but thrice each day   and more than that
    for whenever the israelites go into the synagogues
      and schoolhouses   the holy one   blessed be he
      shakes his head and says

    happy is the king who is thus praised in his house
  woe to the father who had to banish his children
and woe to the children who had to be banished
    from the table of their father

6

        then in the eleventh year of zedekiah s reign
          the wall of the city was breached
        & all the men of war fled by night
            by way of the gate
    between the two walls by the king s garden
                &
    the king went by the way of the arabah

7

as the silver cord trembled
the light from the candle   flickered
the sound of the grinding fell faint
& so the signal
was extinguished *forever*

8

stood in the shadow of
metatron s   kitchen
    smelt
    bitter basalt
amethyst / brewis stewed

    love
tainted by god s intercalated knowledge

    so they scattered seed-pods
       & carved luminous roots
          into destitute earth

9

  stood
in the physic garden of *bergen-belsen*
     cast off shoes from the dead
  furrowed coats
    ploughed
      hopes mutilated wounds
        harrowed dreams
          they dared not dream

  heard
    waves
murmur   distant

10

       stood alone
  under times broken accordion
then with perfectly manicured white polished fingers
bent down low & plucked an orchid from the side of the road

11

the
solid
grey
chimney

becomes
the
sign
of
the
soap
made
from
factories
distilling
adipocere

the soap that he used
when he scrubbed the hand that was stained
because he had jabbed at the jaw of the jew

12

forgot
how her bright white dress
shone through smoke-filled rooms
men laughing
at old jokes

cloaked
bodhrán noised
bodraged tradition

infectious mirth
of *starr*
white space
still
promised
eternity

13

came alive
whenever
he glimpsed her
crossing the road
or threading her way through
stars embedded stone

was it
a mistake to
have calculated his love
by another s inflection

14

fermented rose
dried
red wine
milked
soured-milk of happiness

stood on his body
as it lay out-stretched /
on the floor
& then

       slowly   danced
        on its corps
    with her golden shoes
     trumpets swaying
   drums of eloquence

15

            then they captured zedekiah
and brought him before the king of babylon at riblah
                   and put him on trial
    then they slaughtered his sons before his very eyes
             then they put out his eyes
        and chained him in bronze fetters
          and brought him to babylon

16

now rabbi johanan said
  on the authority of rabbi simeon ben yohai
    that the holy one   blessed be he
  desired to hurl the world back into chaos
    because of zedekiah s generation
but then he gazed at zedekiah and his mind was appeased

    but in the case of zedekiah it is also written
    that he did that which was evil in the sight of god
which means that zedekia could have stemmed the evil of others
      but did not

XXI

  the night-heart s beauty
    is itself enclosed
  adorned in scarlet robes
      &

wrapped around in beautiful silks
    but its tables are broken
  & the once holy tongue
    pierced
   with
dark impossibilities

aglow with fires triumphant
  & its cold steel tempered

words that once adhered to holiness
  are now written
in sikra gum-ink ink-dye & calcanthum

    egyptian / median / aramaic / elamitic / greek

   desiderata
found in eternal pillars of cloud & smoke

  so he wrote in his note-book
   i ishmael son of elisha
did read the book and tilt the lamp on the sabbath

so they asked him
  not to forget to ask of his god
    if their souls would be damned

then he ordered the builders to bury the book inside
  the walls of his house

so they asked him
  whether his faith
   was like
    the bird that sat
     on the roof-top
    of the synagogue of
the coppersmiths of jerusalem

                    but first
          he must cut all the divine names   out of the book
             so that he might conceal them
       inside the palanquin   with its interiors inlaid with love

       so they asked him
             whether his heart had ever perched
       upon the iron honeycombed dome of the temple
          or had sat in the company of the ravens
                 that sing   madness cravings
                 emblazoned
              upon mistletoe

                 then
       he tossed all the falsehood of blank pages
       into the hurricanes that howl through gaza & lebanon
              & blew on the embers
                 until smoke swallowed its fire

                 then
       he gathered all the eighty five letters
             (including all the blank spaces)
       &
       setting his face against the wilderness
              cast them out
          into the vineyards of learning

          so they asked him
                 whether the holy manuscript was torn
                    like the ridge around a field
                    or like a footprint in the dust

             & when he still refused to answer them
                 they asked him
          why the scrolls of the law closed themselves
                    at their middle
              &

    why the writings of the law always finished
              in the middle
       of   a line

and when he still refused to answer   even this
          they asked him
    why the holy name   blessed be he
was never concealed inside the twig
      that bent the hazel sky

but   his silence   opened   like a smile
    that skimmed the space held fast
    inside the presence of something
        not yet mentioned

XXII

    bucklers /   collard of words

     shining light extinguished
       from burning light

      eviscerated dreams
         drawn
    from self-presence-ing
     predicates of language

rotten prelates principled prayers manacled
    perpendicular predilections
       for sex

  flenched/ anger
    reciprocity
of prescient danger
plunged plangent daggers deeper
    into gods paradox

softly spoken
    sweet schemata
        of incardinate shame
    circular thoughts shackled
      sortals lanterns
slatterns symbols & signs

     prescindent rainbows shrouded
    vowels wrapped around bright veneers
      leaning
    leeward

    faith
flashing hope from the bow

    ledden grey waves
      triggered fear
        ignited
      writhled / pastoral flame
   spread wind-fall by day & by night

   stalked
    blighted kestrel s   flight
      hovered over oath oasis & harbour

XXIII

1

once upon a time
in warsaw a construction worker found a milk-can buried
under rubble
on looking inside he found a bundle of manuscripts with a
letter asking that the packet be sent to the author s brother
these were the sermons that rabbi shapira delivered
in the ghetto during the winter of 1942 to 1943

2

      five voices
      flowered

        words
        murmured
    what lies below   between the below
        but can still yield
                its fruit

light of white cloud   turned black into grey

        red latticed sky
the colour of fruit segmented from skin

    the green myrtle veil
      that severed the canopy
    under which she sleeps

what was taken away was the same as was given

3

    historical notation   friday of *parashat vayehi* 1942
      he lived in a time of great trouble
heaven forbid   in this last week the old age home in *patronka*
  where the aged were brought several days earlier
  was completely burned   the old people gathered
in great fear and confusion in the dining room   it is possible
    that the pious woman the daughter of rabbi zalman spitzer
              may his merit protect us
    was among those burned
in the same day the evil ones   may their memory be obliterated
came to the synagogues *temimei derekh* synagogue and others
    and beat the jews who were praying there
        may god have mercy

4

    cold   earth flung from mundane graves
                hard bittern sod
no sound
  to be found
    in the voice that
      scented the blossom
        that opened
          the seventy five palm-trees
            nourished by
              the twelve springs of life

5

    then jacob called his twelve sons and said
come together that i may tell you what will befall you

    unstable as water
slayer of men and maimer of oxen
    a lion s whelp
    a haven for ships
      a toiling serf
        a serpent by the road / a viper by the path
      a raider   raiding at the heels of raiders
        a yielder of royal dainties
          a yielder of lovely fawns
        a wild ass by a spring
          a ravenous wolf

6

first let him deliberate upon the law
then upon the letters of the law
then let him stand at the oaken letterns
built by his father
so that he might rail

against the reigns of heathen imagination
& proclaim the letters-patent
seized
from the *minims* sun-bronzed hands

7

one day rabbi yehudah fell asleep under a tree
and saw   in his dream   four wings arrayed
and rabbi shim'on ascending on them with a *torah* scroll

rabbi shim'on left behind no book of mysteries or aggadah
            but took them away with him

they took him up to heaven and he saw him disappear from sight
        revealed no more   when he awoke rabbi yehudah said
surely ever since rabbi shim'on took his final sleep
            wisdom has departed from the earth
        woe to the generation that has lost this precious stone
            joining upper and lower pillars

8

the wood that they tossed into the ocean
        was like the god that they carved
            from libations of blood

        ten saplings
    woven from the willow of the brook

but   tell me
    would you still wish to be labouring
        under the tale of bricks
    laid out under the
            urgent lash
                of your taskmasters
                    whips

100

XXIV

1

crave not the table of kings
   for their tables are empty
and become like a snare

let the watchman repair
the five tables of broken wood
& the seven tables of stone

let him loose the stuttering tongues
   still bound by satan s scarlet thread
   but do not let him
   knock upon your father s grave
     lest our enemies
steal his soul retrospectively

2

first let us speak the forty-eight names
    deduced by analogy

then let us write upon writing
with the instruments of writing
   drawn from the ark
and from the mouth of the well

   &
    then
let us sanctify
  that distinguished name
   with all the subsidiary names
     embroidered
    on tables prepared
      with pots all around

3

    when we spat out the five pomegranate seeds
    only two of the pips split open behind the crimson veil

       you may look at the likeness of his likeness
       but do not look at the likeness itself

  here is a table corresponding to the table
           just like the tablet
      gamaliel hung on the wall

4

    ninth aspect
        north
    thirteenth month prolonged
      first by   word
      then by deed

  black ink infested the print-makers dowl
    blood bled from the stroke of the scribe
as he scratched at the face of the moon

5

    old bones
        whittled
         sisal nylon linen   & thread
        pigment of skin
      segue segments

incised flesh from the sheaves of the barley once strewn/

    hyssop
       asperged
     raw canvas engorged

that night the king could not sleep
so he ordered the book of records to be brought and read to him

whereupon shamshai the scribe
started to read   from the book
with its writings still being written

memories /

massacres
& callipers
of fear stitched into clouds

your handful of fine flour

6

honi the circle drawer slept for seventy years
but when he awoke no one would believe him

7

napalm not named by god
but sprung from god

not god in bonds abolished

his pen
as gentle as the reed

star shine /   calomel
broken spheres
vengeance suckled
on escharotic
sphincters
of
time

the holy one   blessed be he
wished to appoint hezekiah as the
messiah and sennacherib as gog and
magog whereupon
the attribute of justice said before
the holy one   blessed be he
sovereign of the universe if you did
not make david the messiah who
uttered so many hymns and psalms
before you   will you now appoint
hezekiah as such
who did not hymn you in spite of all
these miracles which you wrought
for him
     therefore the matter was closed
but straightway the earth exclaimed
sovereign of the universe let me
utter song before you instead of
hezekiah so you can make him the
messiah   so the earth broke into
song before the holy one
     then the prince of the universe
said to him   sovereign of the
universe the earth has fulfilled your
desire for songs of praise on behalf
of this righteous man
     but a heavenly voice cried out
it is my secret it is my secret
to which the prophet rejoined
woe is me woe is me
how long must we wait

[BT Sanhedrin 94a (630–631)]

book four

at the gates of paradise

But let him that glorieth glory in this,
That he understandeth and knoweth Me.
[Jeremiah 9:23]

XXV

1

    rabbi samuel ben inia said in the name of rab
        the holy one   blessed be he   has a place
                                and its name is secret

      rabbi eleazar said   why does jeremiah
        make three expressions of tears
   one for the first temple   one for the second temple
and one for israel   who has become exiled from their land

       but there are some who say
   one for the neglect of the study of *torah*

    there are names which may be erased
   and there are names which may not be erased

  our sages taught
     that which is joined to the name
  whether before it or after it   may be erased
   others say
the suffix may not be erased for the name has already hallowed it
rabbi huna said that the *halachah* is in accordance with these others

2

  heart forged / *rem*-silvered silence
     rent   paraclete
   built into temple mount

ashmedai   prince of demons
   cast metaphors visions
     purified   by fire
   purged   plenitudes grace
  suckled   from gods transparent eye

    parabolic
        oversight
of blind sagenite seers
            sagitta sight

        ravens
        hovered
            over
lover s seraglio shadow

    autarchic choirs   angelic eloquence
putrefied the once   triangulated throne

      orion turned   black into white
           triptolemus

3

      miriams song
  fashioned from timbers of cedar
emblazoned upon war s emasculate blood

      misericord
      of plane-song
   /   /
    solid armiger bound

4

      let the earth hear my words
    so that my thoughts might be distilled
just like the dew that nurtures young growth

    &
    let my desires fall as the rains
        that nourish new grass

5

       trochilus   staggered over ragged   eyrie

  built
     bruit
        catalectic
            breath

emblems of desire
prescient siserary
esteemed
  syneidesis

paschal /
braggart grizzled lamb
  brooks not *trochaic* poetry
     but bent   seven cubits
    through   trochus creature delight

6

so what if that odd fellow of
   god s consortium
should always not yet have come
    decked forever
  in his vacuous crowns
   of carved universals
    whilst still hoarding
wreckage upon wreckage

7

cut credence according to crescasian intervals
        electrons of fire
          sparkled
               on the gates of burnished brass

it was said that
no hammer nor axe
nor any iron tool
was ever heard in the house

aniconic
    vultures
  fed on
wingèd plaint

    mother s grief devoured in the wailing

       & then he
   stretched upwards
     his body curved & ringed around
      the wheel within the wheel

  the seventh heaven churned
spurned rebellions eternal brute noise lengthened

8

when ashmedai walked in the footsteps of the messiah
  he opened the pit and found it full of wine

awake awake

9

  agon of artesian emissary
crookèd mouth/   twisted
    tongue
     cleft
to heathen lands

  maggot infested lines
stretched along the perpendicular

        bright vitreous reflux
of indeterminate knowledge
            craved

           then herod
placed a garland of hedgehog bristles
    around the head of ben buta
              &
   depriving him of death
       put out his eyes

10

                     in early may 1944
                in the ghetto of *cehu-silvanie*
            shlomoh zalman ehrenreich
     the eighty-one year old rabbi of *simleul-silvaniei*
                       was caught praying
so they strung him up on a tree until he became unconscious
            then they cut off his beard and *peot*
and seizing the manuscript of his extensive commentary on the
       pirkei avot   they burnt it before his very eyes

        some two weeks later rabbi ehrenreich
                    was transported
                        to auschwitz
where on arrival he was immediately murdered
    with most of the other jews from the ghetto
who were too debilitated to be taken for forced labour

11

   loquacious bacchanalian   number
logaoedic song
   denied
plenitudes principles
   of grace

      lochia
drips from deracinate tears
     reflected
white celestial stone

   pavements of sapphire
carved from laughter s divinity

    idols
  desecrated
     oceans
    of
adamantine bitterness

then the children of dan took whatever micah had made
and together with micah s priest
they came to laish
unto a people quiet and secure
and the children of dan smote them with the edge of the sword
and burnt their city with fire
and there was no deliverer because laish was far from zidon
and the people of laish had no dealings with any man

12

in that day the lord will whistle to the flies at the ends of the water channels of egypt and to the bees in the land of assyria and they shall all come and alight in the rugged wadis and in the clefts of the rocks and in all the thornbrakes and in all the watering places

13

  of the messiah
    ulla said
   let him come
but let me not see him

      the rabbis
called him the leper scholar
      for it is written
that he has born our griefs carried our sorrows
      &
is smitten of god and afflicted

      but hillel the brother of judah said
        may god forgive him
that there will be no messiah for israel
for they have already enjoyed him in the days of hezekia

14

  axioms   adrift
     purloined
      angels
      seared
messianic dreams

    apeiron
of shoas & shadows

burnt flesh /   brittle skin

    larkspur

  white marbled halls

    heft
       from

aporias cognitive complexity

Rabbi Nehorai
used to say:
'Despise not
any
man
and
discriminate
not
against
anything
for
there
is
no man
that has not
his hour
and
there is no thing
that has not
its place.'

[BT Aboth 4:3
(44–45)]

afterwords

We must behave as if the soul were immortal and as if God existed
[Levinas 2000:65]

1

Maimonides' *The Guide of the Perplexed* was the original ur-text / or proof text for twenty-four of the twenty-five sections of this long poem: but two other works also significantly informed its writing

The *Babylonian Talmud* & The *Tanakh*

the *Tanakh*, better known as the Old Testament, comprises *Torah* (the five books of Moses), *Nevi'im* (the Prophets) & *Kethuvim* (the Writings) the *Talmud* comprises the *Mishnah* & *Gemara* and was redacted between c. 400–600 of the Common Era (CE)

my decision not to occlude the voluminous end-notes in this edition was, in part at least, a conditioned reflex from many years working as an historian. but the complex nature of these texts also impelled me to leave traces of the footprints i made as i tramped about the outer margins of talmudic readings. such signs serve not only as markers on the labyrinthine paths that i have travelled but also as ariadnean threads, or maybe gossamer clews, for those readers who might wish to re-trace some (or all) of my paths back to their source(s)

but this foot-printing also has another purpose for it helps to make manifest something of the collagenous nature of this work and its various relationship(s) to the subject matters with which it deals.

at maimonides table is, therefore, my first faltering attempt at a rather informal re-figuration of the old Jewish (medieval) technique of *shibbutz*—the interweaving of biblical and/or talmudic allusions & quotations into the trajectories & parabolas of more prosaic narratives. and it is precisely this matter of *shibbutz* which has helped me explore relationships between different genres & themes thereby allowing me to layer stories & traditions into stories & traditions; and this, in turn, has implications for the readings of these texts.

the *Babylonian Talmud*, from which i have drawn extensively, might be described as the *Gemara* reading the *Mishnah*. but the *Gemara* is not just a series of commentaries on the *Mishnah*, whose order it follows, it is also a complex patterning of a series of meditations upon the *Mishnah's* relationship to and the *Mishnah's* readings of the *Tanakh*.

there is a tradition that the *Mishnah* was first redacted in Palestine under the inspiration of Rabbi Judah ben Simeon, also known as Judah the Prince, or more simply as *Rabbi*, and that his work was completed around the year 220 CE – that is to say some 85 years after the fall of Bethar and some 150 years after the destruction of the second Temple.

in brief the *Mishnah* is primarily a collection of the Halachic or legal teachings gathered from those Rabbis who functioned from the time of Hillel, 30 BCE, to the time of Rabbi, 219 CE, and might therefore be considered as a written record of the ancient Jewish Oral Traditions and thus the most important source of Jewish Law & Lore after the *Tanakh*.   or to put it another way the *Mishnah* is the first extant coherent & comprehensive digest of & commentary on those legal rulings (Halachah) which had been taught through the generations by the old sages (Tannaim) following their own readings & discussions of the *Tanakh*.   as for the *Tanakh* it is, quite simply, *the book* to be read, particularly by the orthodox, as the oral/ written/ oral record of Israel's direct spiritual and historical relationship with Elohim/ Yahweh in so far as that relationship was mediated through her prophets, judges, kings & scribes.

Rabbi Moshe ben Maimon (1138 to 1204), otherwise known as Maimonides or the **Rambam**, believed in the existence of Elohim/ Yahweh, held the *Torah* to be divine revelation and *Nevi'im* (the Prophets) & *Kethuvim* (the writings) as divinely inspired.

the Rambam first established his reputation as a scholar and rabbinical leader and then as the author of the *Mishneh Torah*, his own impressive codification of, and commentary on, the *Mishnah*.   Rambam's *Mishneh Torah* still holds sway even today.   but when Maimonides came to write *The Guide of the Perplexed*, sometime around 1190, he had in mind something quite different from his previous strictly theological and ethical writings.   for in writing the *Guide* Maimonides sought to bring together, or accommodate, two bodies of thought, which at the outset seemed entirely unrelated.   on the one hand Jewish revelation and tradition, which existed as a body of authoritative texts, and on the other hand that body of Greek-Arabic rational thought which had been systematized by the great representatives of Arabic Aristotelianism.   or to quote Leo Straus: the aim of Maimonides was to establish a "true science of the *Torah*". it was this aspect of the Rambam's work that served as the starting point for my researching and writing these texts.

2

this book started as a series of draft poems which i wrote between early September and late December 2003. as i neared completion of what would turn out to be a first draft, i noticed a number of recurring threads which suggested that the poems might relate to each other thematically as well chronologically. on further reading i began to wonder how these writings might relate to Maimonides' more philosophical speculations. but as my knowledge of the Rambam's work was even more fragmentary than it is today i was unable to take those speculations any further. what is more i was deeply engrossed in researching *The Unturned Stone: letters from Bamberg 1938–1941*, a closely annotated edition of my (paternal) grandparents' letters to their eldest son (my uncle) who had fled Germany for America in June 1938.

although i finally finished *The Unturned Stone* in late March 2005 it was not until some nine months later, following the death of my father Martin, that i first started to sense how i might fashion those poems into a coherent whole. and while this book is not about the death of my father its very foundations – from the intense research through its numerous revisions – have clearly been constrained within that psychical space of emotional turmoil that followed my experiencing my father's dying and the subsequent presence of his death. but it was perhaps, above all, my participation in the extraordinary ritual of his burial, conducted according to the ancient & orthodox precepts of his synagogue's *chevra kadisha* (burial society), which ultimately impelled me to confront, once again, that tradition of Judaism which had formed & informed such an important part of my childhood and which now began to infiltrate the revisions of these texts.

as this work neared completion i began to think of its numerous sections as deltas, continually spreading outwards towards some impossible end. as if the various threads of these texts had been nourished by artesian wells, tributaries, streams, channels, rivers, gullies, and water courses, all of which might ultimately be traced back to that single ineffable source: the original encounter between God & Moses on mount Sinai. at times it seemed possible to follow this source through one of the text's slow meandering streams, at other times it seemed as if that same source threatened to overwhelm the very writings that it was supposed to irrigate.

this metaphor-of-water might at first appear to be a rather strained conceit: but i think that it helps to illustrate one of the themes that twists through this work – those conundrums that arise when one holds to, or believes in, a theophany that embraces earthly salvation through imminent redemption.

from time to time rabbis quoted in the *Babylonian Talmud* seem to use metaphors, or images, of water as a means of articulating their own responses to the non-appearance of the messiah. this, in turn, suggests readings for metaphors of water, or perhaps more specifically, readings for rabbinical a/(i)llusions to water, through those four exegetical registers referred to as **PRDS** – **P**eshat (literal readings), **R**amez (allusive or allegorical readings), **D**erasha (solicited or talmudic readings) and **S**od (secret or mystical readings). such provocations help to highlight some of the aporias that open when a messianic doxology engages with the belief in the possibility of entering into paradise here on earth & in the *here-and-now*. for there is a powerful strain of rabbinical thought which believes that one can enter into, or inhabit, an earthly paradise (or **PaRaDiSe** as it would be transliterated from Hebrew) through the performance of good deeds. this includes not only righteous actions, such as acts of charity and strict religious observances, but also, crucially, the active reading and studying of **Torah**. book two of this poem, with its four meditations upon the Talmudic "story" of the four who entered the garden (**PRDS**), is a faltering attempt to explore some of the implications that flow from such teachings and, in this respect at least, is also an attempt to articulate that still (im)possible "ethics of .... messianic faith".

but such coincidental disclosures and concealments of meaning, which the use of metaphor can so neatly encapsulate, also echoes that strange Jewish reticence about speaking too directly about one's longing for redemption. and yet this longing lies at the very heart of Judaism and twists, like a golden thread, through many aspects of her theology, philosophy, liturgy & literature. to offer just one example: the **Kaddish** which is not just the prayer of mourning but also a significant component of the Jewish liturgy has, amongst its opening lines, this fervent wish: that "(God's) Kingship be established *in your lifetime* and *in your days* and in the lifetime of the entire household of Israel *swiftly and in the near future* and say amen".

this certain-uncertain anticipation of the messiah who will have always not yet have come but who might still arrive at any second can also be traced through the works of countless modern Jewish writers: Marx, Freud, Rosenzweig, Bloch, Kafka, Benjamin, Buber, Sperber & Levinas to name just a few.

for my own part i have woven metaphors of water through some of the fragmentary narratives of these texts in order to try to sketch & explore some of the paradoxes woven into this messianic discourse-of-immanence. the "wippen waters", "the caverns of paneas", and the water of bitterness", are just a few examples: whilst the borrowing of the "rivers that failed" is an implicit, not to say explicit, reference to rabbinical comments concerning *Shimon bar Kokhbah*'s messianic uprising which seems to have convinced even Rabbi Akiba for a short time at least, or until Kokhbah's revolt was brutally suppressed by the Romans at Bethar in 135 CE.

at maimonides table might be read as a series of meditations loosely bound by a number of specifically Jewish events, themes and/or myths. i might mention, for example, the significance of the book, the love of learning *Torah*, a unique type of relationship with "god", the importance of memorialization and the (quite different) significance of memory. and then there are, of course, those defining catastrophic events which have so shaped Jewish sensibilities such as: the defeat at Megiddo, the betrayal at Mizpah, the Babylonian exile, the destruction(s) of the first and second Temple(s), the martyrdom of the ten rabbis, the defeat at Bethar, to say nothing of the countless massacres, pogroms and exiles which (for the moment at least) culminate in *Shoah* (the Holocaust) that singular event which also masquerades under the signs of Auschwitz, Belzec, Sobibor, Treblinka, Bergen-Belsen, Dachau

    although each of these 25 chapters engages with matters which are often deeply embedded in some collective Jewish psyche of remembrance, i hope that they can also be read and thought-through in non-denominational ways. this hope springs from my belief that these "jewish" stories of triumph and tragedy, wisdom and humility, which often contain a kind (of) self-deprecating humour, can also resonate beyond the Jewish imagination and thereby speak to those others who have also endured, directly or vicariously, those all too common experiences of oppression, persecution, exile, pogrom, & genocide, to say nothing of all those other pointless mundane murders carried out in the names of god-knows-who & god-knows-what.

this book has grown out of a series of difficult engagements and confrontations with my jewishness, with my uncertain relationship to that jewish-ness, with my very being of jewishness

    a stranger in a strange land   and yet i trust that these (auto)biographical meditations might also spread outwards and thereby enter into that wider debate concerning how we, both collectively and as individuals, might better understand how to become our selves in peaceful relationships with others. how through those all too fleeting moments of our meetings, be they in person or now increasingly mediated through screens, we can begin to engage with those dilemmas which exercise and trouble all of us who still passionately care about protecting and promoting all that is sacred, both within the sacred and the mundane. to offer a very different orientation to the self-serving hypocrisies of those who would try to cloak their murderous ambitions and obscenities under the guises of religion, progress, wealth, efficiency, freedom or even (*god help us*) democracy.

    Buckfastleigh
    29 september 2008 / 29 elul 5768

notes

Chapter I

But if we explain these parables to him or if we draw his attention to their being parables, he will take the right road and be delivered from this perplexity. [Maimonides 1:6]

p.8. "hillel the elder …", [BT] *Sukkah* 53a (253).
"the eagle of córdoba", Maimonides.
"scourge of tongue", *Job* 5:21.
"a dance of two companies", reference to *Song of Songs* 7:1.

p.9. "jacob s covetous stall", the allusion here (and in the remainder of this first section) is to the defeat of Shimon bar Kokhbah at Bethar (c. 135 ce): "the deceitful brooks", "rivers that fail", "liar", & "star" are all allusions to the false messianic promises made by Kokhbah and are based on Rabbinical readings of *Jeremiah* 15:18 & *Job* 6:15.

Chapter II

The Sage accordingly said that a saying uttered with a view to two meanings is like an apple of gold overlaid with silver filigree-work having very small holes. Now see how marvellously this dictum describes a well-constructed parable. [Maimonides 1:12]

p.11. "as pale as silver …", *Psalm* 12:7.

Chapter III

… we do not know nor can we represent to ourselves how a notion can be transmitted from the soul of one individual who is among us to the soul of another individual except through the instrumentality of speech, which is sound produced by the lips, the tongue and other organs of speech. [Maimonides 1:98]

p.11 "the god that squashed …", reference to *Kierkegaard* 1985:41–42n.
p.12 "the narrow streets of luz", [BT] *Sotah* 46b (242).
"scanners / cutters of heavens …", *Isaiah* 47:13.
"Regulus", Regulus M. Attilius a consul during the first Punic War.

p.13. "the rod of their mouth/the breath of their lips", *Isaiah* 11:4.
"when i am reproved", *Habakkuk* 2:1 (*variant reading*).
"of tigers /slaughtered ...", *Deuteronomy* 32:24; & *[BT] Pesahim* 111b (573).
p.14. "jacobs star", a veiled reference to *bar Kokhbah*.
"... covered with figs", *[BT] 'Erubin* 54b (379). The fig tree is often read as a metaphor for *Torah*.
p.15. "... in the arms of sarah", *[BT] Baba Bathra* 58a (233).
"... i have dreamed", *Jeremiah* 23:25.
"*al-andalus*", the medieval Iberian peninsula; see i.e., *Anidjar* 2002.
p.16. "... and ruthless mob", *Levinas* 1996:123.

Chapter IV

I refer to the notion of providence watching over human individuals according to the measure of their perfection and excellence.
[Maimonides 2:476]

"green porcelain sky", reference *Rilke* 1992:150, *Duineser Elegien* 8,
"... So reißt die Spur/ der Fledermaus durchs Porzellan des Abends."
p.18. "purling well of sound", *Scholem* 1972:170.

Chapter V

For the nature of impossibility is stable and cannot be abolished, as we shall make clear. [Maimonides 2:303]

p.19. "watchman what of the night", *Isaiah* 21:11.
"the sound of the horn ...", *[BT] Rosh Hashanah* 29b (138).
"if the morning cometh ...", *Isaiah* 21:12.
"a lamp at my feet", from Nahmanides, "Before the World Ever Was", in *Cole* 2007:235.
"set me upon the tower", *Habakkuk* 2:1.
p.20. "the rip of a dice", reference *[BT] Yoma* 39b (186).
"read it swiftly/ ... for it will surely come", *Habakkuk* 2:2, 2:3.
"... sealed it with his name", *Scholem* 1972:69–70.

Chapter VI

Now you know that the principles of the existents subject to generation and corruption are three: Matter, Form and Particularised Privation, which is always conjoined with Matter. For, were it not for this conjunction with Privation, Matter would not receive Form. [Maimonides 1:43]

p.21. "... silent and audible voice", Scholem 1972:184.
"moaning ... tabouring upon her breast", *Nahum* 2:8.
"... ploughed as a field", *Micah* 3:12.
"when *judah ben baba* ...", *[BT] Sanhedrin* 14a (63–64).

p.22. "litotes", understatement .
"bright white spot on the hand ...", *[M] Nega'im*, chp. 2:1.
"the white of the eye", *[BT] Gittin* 56a (254–255).
"the ten places of banishment", *[BT] Rosh Hashanah* 31a–31b (149).
"... departed the fruit", *[BT] Sotah* 48a (256).
"littoral", belonging to the seashore.

p.23. "tress", a plait, a braid of hair but also the *challah* – a sweet, golden egg-bread often used on festive occasions.
"the ovens of akhnai", *[BT] Baba Mezi'a* 59b (352). Scholem 1995:291f.

p.24. "though your sins be crimson ...", *Isaiah* 1:18.
"knock this nail ...", *Ezra* 9:8 [variant reading].
"a keeping to my keeping ...", *[BT] Yebamoth* 21a (124).
"the voice that sings in the window", *[BT] Sotah* 48a (257).
"then the king of babylon ...", *Jeremiah* 52:26.

p.25. "dweller on the frontier", *[BT] Sotah* 49b (267).
"the assiduous student at *jabneh*", *[BT] 'Erubin* 13b (85).
"protect the orchard ...", reference *[BT] Yebamoth* 21a (123–124).
"engravings of the signet", *Exodus* 28:11.
"so they cut off the branch ...", Nelly Sachs "Chorus of Orphans", in *Celan & Sachs*, 1995:20–21.

p.26. "proskurov" site of anti-semitic pogrom in February 1919 when Ataman Semosenko & his Cossack regiment of Gaidamacs, massacred c. 1600 Jews: "Odessa"; saw pogroms in 1821, 1859, 1871, 1881, 1886 & 1905. "toledo/barcelona" sites of anti-jewish "riots" on 5 August 1391. for "tur malka" & "bethar", see *[BT] Gittin* 57a (261, 264) .
"*gehinnoms*", also Gehenna; the place of punishment for the wicked in the hereafter: *[BT] 'Erubin* (19a) 129f, *[BT] Baba Bathra* 10a (45).
"vessel of finest gold", *[BT] Hagigah* 15a (95); *Job* 28:17.
"megiddo", *2 Kings* 23:29.

Chapter VII

For a privation of providence leaves one abandoned and a target to all that may happen and come about, so that his ill and weal come about according to chance. How terrible is this threat! [Maimonides 1:53]

"cunning ruse of reason", see *Pines* 1963:lxxii.

"csárdás", an Hungarian dance in two movements, slow and fast

"... the rods of the word", *Habakkuk* 3:9.

"through orion", *[BT] Berakoth* 58b (365).

p.27. "howl cypresses ...", *Zechariah* 11:2.

"five parts of your soul", reference *Maimonides* 1975:61.

"i have calculated and made no mistake", *[BT] Megillah* 11b (65).

p.28. "the three keepers of the door", *[BT] Megillah* 23a (139); *2 Kings* 25:18.

"the academy of the sky", *[BT] Gittin* 68a (323).

"like a pillow rolled up", *[BT] Berakoth* 58b (365–366), *[BT] Hullin* 91b (513).

"inside the line of the law", *Maimonides* 1975:30.

"in the heart of the fig", reference *[BT] Shabbath* 90a (430).

"... the buckler and shield", *Jeremiah* 46:3.

"sound the timbrel ...", *Psalm* 81:3–4.

"shimon bar kokhbah ...", Jerusalem Talmud, Ta'anith, in *Montefiore & Loewe* 1938:262.

p.29. "... the sweet harp and the psaltry", *Psalm* 81:3.

"... gathered in our vessels", *Jeremiah* 40:10.

"the well of palm-trees", *[BT] Shabbath* 110a (536), *[BT] Nazir* 51b (191).

"the speech of palm-trees", *[BT] Sukkah* 28a (123).

"bethars city walls ...", reference *[BT] Gittin* 57a–b (264–265).

"the lord said unto job ...", *Job* 38:30–31.

Chapter VIII

Should, however, the man who proclaims these things and attempts to establish them in the ways indicated, reflect upon his belief, he would find nothing but confusion and incapacity. For he wants to make exist something that does not exist and to create a mean between two contraries that have no mean. Or is there a mean between that which exists and that which does not exist ... [Maimonides 1:114].

p.30. "bushido", Japanese code of chivalry.
"contraplex", having messages passing opposite ways at the same time
p.31. "then for three and a half years ...", this version of the fall of Bethar, Jerusalem Talmud, Ta'an, in *Montefiore & Loewe* 1938:263.
"the cities of refuge", *Joshua* 20:1–2.
"the bottomless abyss", *Scholem* 1972:69.
"golden candlestick", refers to Genesis Rabba, in *Montefiore & Loewe* 1938:267.
p.32. "... the twinkling of an eye", *[BT] Berakoth* 2b (5).
"... parchment skins", *[BT] Makkoth* 11a (71).
"the precept of fringes", *[BT] Berakoth* 12b (71).
"a niche in his own grave", refers to *[BT] Berakoth* 14b (85).
"a clue within a clue", *[BT] Sotah* 13B (72).
"prescribed limit", reference *[BT] Hagigah* 7a (31).
"sorrow from each generation", reference *[BT] Makkoth* 11a (73).
"plaited wreaths of her golden hair", *Song of Songs* 1:10, & "Death Fugue", *Celan* 2001:31.
"viaticum", money or provisions for a journey: or the Eucharist given to persons in danger of death.

Chapter IX

Similarly in all cases in which there is no likeness between two things, there is no relation between them. An example of this is that one does not say that this heat is like this colour, or that this voice is like this sweetness. This is a matter that is clear in itself. ... it follows necessarily that likeness between Him and us should also be considered nonexistent. [Maimonides 1: 130]

p.33. "... carried him to babylon", *2 Kings* 25:5–7.
"similor", a yellow alloy used in cheap jewellery.
"i am your sign", *Ezekiel* 12:11 [variant reading].
"... the word of every vision", *Ezekiel* 12:23.
"an idol was placed in the temple", *[BT] Ta'anith* 26b (138–139).
p.34. "... burnt them in fire", *[BT] Gittin* 58a (270).
"their own prayer shawls", reference *[BT] Gittin* 57b (267–268).
"the city of jerusalem/ploughed up", *[BT] Ta'anith* 26b (139).

"the trap with no corn", *[BT] Pesahim* 119a (614).

"the cavern of paneas", *[BT] Baba Bathra* 74b (297). R. Jose b. Kisma hints at a relationship between the grotto of Paneas and Messiah, see *[BT] Sanhedrin* 98a (665). The river Jordan is said to issue from the cavern of Paneas in Caesarea Philippi (modern Banias in the north of Galilee), *[BT] Bekoroth* 55a (377).

"the blood that flows ...", reference to the slaughter at Bethar, *[BT] Gittin* 57a (264).

"cast it into the deep", *[BT] Sukkah* 53b (256), *[BT] Makkoth* 11a (74)

"our bones are dried up ...", *Ezekiel* 37:11.

p.35. "inside the sepulchre ...", *[BT] Menahoth* 189n5.

"a vessel of papyrus", reference *Isaiah* 18:2.

"... in its waters", reference *Numbers* 5:23–24.

"the wheel that never stops turning", reference *[BT] Baba Bathra* 74a (294).

"in the shadow of god", *[BT] Berakoth* 55a (336).

"Boaz", the husband of Ruth, *Ruth* 4:13.

"cradled gazelle ...", *Song of Songs* 2:1, 7:1, 7:7; & "Death Fugue", Celan 2001:30.

Chapter X

These subtle notions that very clearly elude the minds cannot be considered through the instrumentality of the customary words, which are the greatest among the causes leading unto error. For the bounds of expression in all languages are very narrow indeed, so that we cannot represent this notion to ourselves except through a certain looseness of expression. [Maimonides 1;132–133]

p.36. "azimuth", the arc of the horizon between the meridian of a place and a vertical circle passing through any celestial body.

"azoth", the alchemists' name for mercury – Paracelsus's universal remedy.

Chapter XI

I mean the multiplicity of opinions, the variety of schools, the confusions occurring in the expression of what is put down in writing, the negligence that accompanies what is written down, the divisions of the people, who are separated into sects, and the production of confusion with regard to actions. [Maimonides 1:175–176]

p.37. "coniine", highly poisonous alkaloid found in hemlock.
"lancinate", to lacerate, to pierce.
"laniary", fitted for tearing. Also a butcher.
"if she be a wall ...", *Song of Songs* 8:9.
"linger in the garden ...", *Song of Songs* 8:13.
"... the citadels of shushan", *Daniel* 8:2.

p.38. "faburdened", harmony in thirds & sixths: an early kind of counterpoint.
"... demanding hellenism", "Of the Jews (50AD)", *Cavafy* 2001:105
"evil waters", *[M] Avoth* chp 1:11 (493). A reference to Hellenistic thought.
"his master s ear", reference *[BT] Kiddushin* 21b (101f).

p.39. "enucleated", deprive of a kernel or nucleus: to explain.
"at riblah", *2 Kings* 25:4–7.
"burnt the house of the lord ...", *2 Kings* 25:8–9.

Chapter XII

p.42. "the mouth of ... seventy-two elders", *[BT] Zebahim* 11b (58).
"hectic", pertaining to constitution or habit of body; feverish agitated. But also a play on *heck* a euphemism for hell: also an inner door.
"the drum ...", *[BT] Sotah* 49a (265). During the war with Vespian the Rabbis decreed against the use of the drum at wedding festivals.
"rendered it invalid", reference *[BT] Kinnim* chp. 3:6 (22–23n).
"the one who erred" reference *[BT] Horayoth* 2b (6–7).
"cimolion earth", species of clay or fullers earth, *[BT] Nazir* 65a (246).

p.43. "write upon writing", reference *[BT] Shabbath* 104b (503).
"cast by the waves of the sea", a reference to the appearance of Herod's Temple in Jerusalem, *[BT] Sukkah* 51b (244).
"the gates of weeping", *[BT] Berakoth* 32b (199).
"hover on water", reference *[BT] Hagigah* 15a (92), *Deuteronomy* 32:11.
"secreting liquid myrrh", *reference* [BT] *Shabbath* 30b (136).

p.44. "all the blank spaces ...", *[BT] Shabbath* 116a (569).

"break the bones", *Proverbs* 25:15.

"Elisha ben Abuyah", because of his uncertain status Elisha is usually referred to as *Aher*, meaning The Other.

"the thirteen souls ...", reference *[BT] Kiddushin* 39b (194–195), *[BT] Hagigah* 15a–b (95–96).

"behind the veil", *[BT] Hagigah*15a–b (95–96).

"a window in the sky", *[BT] Sanhedrin*, 100b (680).

"lick the dust", reference to Aher's apostacy, *[BT] Hagigah* 15a (95).

p.45. "*his* mouth". Some say that Aher's apostasy occured when he saw the tongue of Huzpith the Interpreter draged along by swine, *[BT] Kiddushin* 39b (195). See also *[BT] Hullin* 142a (824–825).

"fly from the fire", *[BT] 'Abodah Zarah* 18a (92), *Scholem* 1969:81–82, *[BT] Hagigah* 15b (100).

"empty martyrs nest", reference *[BT] Hullin* 141b (822).

"when we lay ...", reference to the 'story' told about Akiba's early years; taken from *[BT] Nedarim* 50a (155–156).

"the silver cord ...", reference to rituals for caring for the dead *[BT] Shabbath* 151b (771).

"knotted your thread", reference *[BT] Sotah* 4a (13).

"who kneaded your dough", reference *[BT] Pesahim* 36a (167).

"men of arm ...", *[BT] Sotah* 49a (266).

"pluck up your trees and be gone", *[BT] Baba Bathra* 37a–b, (165).

p.46. "incense balm and embers", reference *[BT] Yoma* 48a (228)

"... no visible end", *[BT] Yebamoth* 121a (856–857).

"hall of hewn stone", *[BT] Sanhedrin* 88b (585).

"... pierce the abyss", reference *[BT] Sanhedrin* 97b (658–659).

"i blotted this out", reference *[BT] 'Erubin* 13a (81–82).

"the bright white blemish ...", this relates to Akiba's mastery of the complex rules for diagnosis and purification of leprosy: see *[BT] Nega'im* ch.1:1–2 (233).

"the broken stool", reference *[BT] 'Eduyyoth* ch. 2:8 & 10 (14).

"the three worlds", reference *[BT] Sanhedrin* 64b (441).

"gentle as the reed", *[BT] Ta'anith* 20b (100–101).

"engraved/ in the fields", reference *[BT] Baba Bathra* 28a (138&n).

p.47. "the soles of my feet", *Malachi* 3:21, but also a reference to the discussion about Gehinnom in *[BT] Rosh Hashanah* 17a (64).

"the eye of the serpent", reference to the story told about Akiba's daughter's wedding night, in *[BT] Shabbath* 156b (801).

"needle of thorns", reference to *[BT] 'Erubin* 53a (370), & *[BT] Abodah Zarah* 46a (226).

"into the mouth of my teachers", reference to *[BT] Shabbath* 67b (323)

"the stripes of my flesh", reference to Akiba's martyr's death borrowed from *[BT] Menahoth* 29b (190).

Chapter XIII

In this way will he who wants to understand the prophetic riddles understand them. And he will awaken from the sleep of negligence, be saved from the sea of ignorance, and rise up toward the high ones. [Maimonides 2:273]

p.50. "wisdom has built her house", *Proverbs* 9:1–2.

"the blank spaces ...", reference *[BT] Shabbath* 116a (569).

p.51. "... seeds sacred dominion", reference *Rosenzweig* 2005:318.

"in the deep shadow ...", *Isaiah* 18:1.

"vineyards fertilised ...", reference *[BT] Gittin* 57a (265).

"the fountain of living waters", *Maimonides* 2:280, *Jeremiah* 2:13.

p.52. "when they camped ...", *Exodus* 17:1–6, *[BT] 'Arakin* 15a (86).

"... the *torah* for israel", *[BT] Yoma* 4a (13).

"broken cisterns that hold no water", *Jeremiah* 2:13.

"gematria the almighty", Sefer Zerubbabel, in *Stern & Mirsky* 1990:73.

"range over the earth", *Psalm* 73:9.

"if a man in a fit of jealousy ...", *Numbers* 5:16–28.

p.53. "a falsehood / of blank pages", *[BT] Shabbath* 116a (571n).

"... write them in dust", reference *[BT] Shabbath* 104b (503).

p.54. "described in her flesh", *[BT] Shabbath* 104b (504).

"noise of grindstones", *[BT] Sanhedrin* 32b (204).

"assembled at *bethar*", reference *[BT] Gittin* 57a (264).

"a net spread out over tabor", *Hosea* 5:1.

p.55. "epicureans", a term of abuse used in the *Talmud* to denote not only Epicurean philosophy but also those who held heretical beliefs, *[BT] Sanhedrin* 90a (602n).

"creance", the cord which secures the hawk in training.

"from the serpents jaw", reference to the story of Cadmus sowing the dead dragon/serpent's teeth, *Gantz* 1996:468f.

"... that already belongs to the fruit", reference *Levinas* 2000:40.

"the libyan ass", reference *[BT] Shabbath* 116a (571).

"books that may not be read", reference *[BT] Shabbath* 116b (572).

"... saved from the fire", reference *[BT] Shabbath*115af (563f).

p.56. "last blast of the horn", *2 Samuel* 15:10.

"rabbi joshua ...", *[BT] 'Erubin* 19a (131–2).

p.57. "dark sayings of the harp", reference *Psalm* 49:5.

"then the officers of the troop ...", *Jeremiah* 40:13–14.

"feasts of crematoriums", *Herzberg* 1997:133.

p.58. "then johanan ...", *Jeremiah* 40:15–16.

"execution by the sword ..." *[BT] Sanhedrin* 52b (354).

p.59. "once the grandfather ...", *[BT] Sanhedrin* 104a (706–7).

"once at kefer saba ...", *[BT] Niddah* 61a (431).

"nets of imagination", reference *Maimonides* 1:210.

p.60. "then in the seventh month ...", *Jeremiah* 41:1–3.

p.61. "nahum the scribe ...", reference *[BT] Pe'ah*. This tractate, *Pe'ah* (corner of the field), mainly concerns questions as to how much of the harvest one must give to the poor.

"now the cistern ...", *Jeremiah* 41:9 .

Chapter XIV

Sometimes one may hear in someone else's speech words that in the language of the speaker indicate a certain meaning, and by accident that word indicates in the language of the hearer the contrary of what the speaker intended. Thus the hearer will think that the signification that the word has for the speaker is the same as its signification for him. [Maimonides 2:336]

p.62. "seven white mules ...", reference *[BT] Pesahim* 119a (613f).

" let the contentious woman ...", *Proverbs* 21:9 & 14.

"phinehas", Aaron's grandson, & therefore Moses's great-nephew, *[BT] Sanhedrin* 82a (546).

"and behold six men ...", *Ezekiel* 9:2. See also *[BT] Shabbath* 55a (254).

"*bamoth*", "The High Place". Before the erection of the Tabernacle at *Shiloh* and then between its destruction and the building of the (first) Temple, sacrifices were offered here. *Bamoth* have been forbidden since the destruction of the Temple, reference *[BT] Pesahim* 91a (486–7).

p.63. "and the lord called ...", *Ezekiel* 9:3–5.
p.64. "remember ...", reference *Weber* 2004b:17.
"integrate those memories", *Vidal-Naquet* 2004:27.
"then from the roof ...", *[BT] Ta'anith* 29a (155).
p.65. "the day of perplexity ...", *Isaiah* 22:5.
"the voice of another", reference *[BT] Sanhedrin* 98a (664).
"speak from the grave", reference *[BT] Sanhedrin* 90b (605).
"the man clothed in linen ...", *Ezekiel* 9:11.

Chapter XV

They also give us a second hint, saying that the word derives from the notions of speech and silence, saying that they sometimes hashoth *[are silent] and sometimes* memalleloth *[speak]. They ascribe the meaning silence [to hash] from the verse:* hehesheiti *[I have been silent] for a long time; there is thus an allusion to two notions through the indication of speech without sound.*
[Maimonides 2:429–430]

"as a precious stone", *[BT] Kiddushin* 22b (106).
"a sigh ...", *[BT] Berakoth* 58b (363): "a seal upon", *Song of Songs* 8:6.
"the fine flour ...", *[BT] Sotah* 48b (261).
p.66. "a certain clod of earth ...", *[BT] Niddah* 61a (432) & *Jeremiah* 41:9.
"rabbi shila once said ...", *[BT] Berakoth* 58a (362), *Exodus* 22:1. See also *[BT] Yoma* 85af (420f).
p.67. "four hundred jars ...", *[BT] Berakoth* 5b (22).
"snapped at their heels", reference *[BT] Shebu'oth* 47b (291).
"pharmaceutics and roots ...", *Maimonides* 1993:24.
"zechariah s scrupulousness ...", *[BT] Gittin* 56a (255).
"a coin into the ocean", *[BT] Baba Kamma* 98a (568).
"a slave to his pen", reference *Maimonides* 1993:15f.
"the shadow of his wing", *Psalm* 36:8.
"in the upper-market at sepphoris", *[BT] Abodah Zarah* 17a (85).
p.68. "dancing ... turned into mourning", *Lamentations* 5:15.
"merry with wine", *Esther* 1:10.
"spoilers of spoilers", reference *[BT] Sanhedrin* 94a (631).
"treacherous dealers", *[BT] Sanhedrin* 94a (631).
"the temple of nimrod", also known as the *Tower of Babel*, reference *[BT] 'Abodah Zarah* 53b (273).

"a tower that flies in the air", *[BT] Hagigah* 15b (99).

"the quivers of lilith", reference *[BT] Gittin* 69b (329).

p.69. "jealousy as cruel as the grave", reference *Song of Songs* 8:6.

"they riddled his body ...", *[BT] Mo'ed Katan* 28b (189).

"then jeremiah said ...", *Jeremiah* 41:16, 42:9–12, 43:1–7; *2 Kings* 25:26

Chapter XVI

On the other hand, men of excellence and knowledge have grasped and understood the wisdom manifested in that which exists, as David has set forth, saying: All the paths of the Lord are mercy and truth unto such as keep His covenant and His testimonies. [Maimonides 2:446]

p.70. "nimos the weaver", also a reference to *Oenomaus* the cynic philosopher, *[BT] Hagigah* 15b (100).

"soft murmuring sound", *1 Kings* 19:12.

"*the burden of dumah*", *[BT] Sanhedrin* 94a (631). *Dumah*, the angel in charge of souls. See also *Isaiah* 21:11.

"valley of visions", reference *Isaiah* 22:1.

"babylonian palaces", reference *[BT] Sanhedrin* 96b (653).

p.71. "the verse that pierced ...", reference *[BT] Sanhedrin* 97b (658).

"the scourge of ... tongue", *Job* 5:21.

"thus said the lord of hosts ...", *Zechariah* 8:23.

"*like a hammer that breaks ...*", *[BT] Shabbath* 88b (420).

p.72. "the words *asher kummetu* ...", *[BT] Hagigah* 14a (82).

"did we not cast three ...", *Daniel* 3:24–25.

"then elijah led *rabbah* ...", *[BT] Baba Metzi'a* 114b (652).

p.73. "the sight of her presence", reference *[BT] Sanhedrin* 97b (659).

"through a bright speculum", *[BT] Sanhedrin* 97b (659).

"the valley of dura", *[BT] Sanhedrin* 92b (621). This relates back to p.72, "*did we not cast three ...*".

"to smell and to judge ...", *[BT] Sanhedrin* 93b (627); *Isaiah* 11:3.

"before then do not expect him ...", *[BT] Sanhedrin* 97b (658).

"blasted be the bones ...", reference *[BT] Sanhedrin* 97a (657f).

"for rabbi torta ...", rabbi Torta's response when Akiba hailed *Bar Kokba* as "King Messiah". Jerusalem Talmud, *Ta'an*, quoted Montefiore & Loewe 1938:262.

Chapter XVII

For since his house is safeguarded and this benefit comes to him because of the ruler, the matter looks as if the final end of the ruler were the safeguarding of the house of that individual. We must interpret in this sense every text whose external sense we find indicates that something sublime has been made for the sake of something inferior to it; this text means that this act follows necessarily from the nature of the sublime. [Maimonides 2:454–5]

p.74. "quarries of the soul", Yehudah Halevi quoted *Wolfson* 1994:180.

p.75. "... scentedhiscoat", reference *[BT] Baba Metzi'a* 114b (652).

"*kokhba*/ the liar/ the star", verbal plays on *Numbers* 24:17 which some thought predicted the coming of Messiah (*Simon bar Kokhbah*) not the fatal Messianic revolt against Hadrian (132–135 CE).

"*phinehas*", a tradition has it that Elijah was Aaron's grandson.

"*alampof...*", *Zohar* 1:86b (2:54).

"intermingled with water", *Zohar* 1:56b (1:318).

"lachesis", one of the three fates: the one who assigns destiny.

"joined into one", reference *Zohar* 1:206b (3:265).

p.76. "*shewa*", a vowel-letter in Hebrew which carries either a silent or a quick vowel-like sound.

"a language to speak ...", *Levinas* 2000:151–156.

"it was broken", reference *[BT] Shabbath* 117b (576).

p.78. "according to josephus ...", *Josephus* 1981:259.

Chapter XVIII

For when man knows his own soul, makes no mistakes with regard to it, and understands every being according to what it is, he becomes calm and his thoughts are not troubled by seeking a final end for what has not that final end; or by seeking any final end for what has no final end except its own existence, which depends on the divine will – if you prefer you can also say: on the divine wisdom. [Maimonides 2:456]

p.78. "josef s prepared table", reference to Joseph Caro's *Shulchan Arukh* (Prepared Table). A summary of *Beth Yosef,* Caro's early sixteenth-century codification of *Halachic* rulings, still functions as a primary source for Orthodox Ashkenazi Jews.

p.79. "the prince", i.e., Judah ben Simeon, compiler of the *Mishnah*.

"rue goosefoot purslane ...", [BT] Shebi'ith chp 9:1 (183).
"a fiery law", reference Deuteronomy 33:2.
"clenched inside his pocket", Bloch 1995:30.
"opens from the right", reference [BT] Shabbath 88b (420).
"... mingled with bread", reference [BT] Terumoth 10:4 (241).

p.80. "let the suspicion of blood ...", Tosefta Sanhedrin quoted in Montefiore & Loewe 1938:241.
"... in times of peace", 1 Kings 2:5.
"crushed in the building", reference [BT] Sanhedrin 101a (688).
"and they blew the horn", 2 Samuel 20:1.
"for rab judah said ...", [BT] Sanhedrin 104a (706).

p.81. "dream of the vine", reference Genesis 40:9–10.
"inspired by the counsel of god", 2 Samuel 16:23.
"then joshua said to ulla", reference to Joshua ben Levi telling Ulla bar Qoosheb that if he (Joshua) refused to surrender Ulla to the Romans then the Romans would execute many hostages. Joshua's actions are discussed in Samuelson 2003:120.
"a rumour was spread ...", [BT] Niddah 61a (432–3).

p.82 "the ovens of aknai", [BT] Berakoth 19a (115).

p.83. "the martyrs of lud", reference [BT] Baba Bathra 10b (50).
"baladan", employed Nebuchadnezzar as a scribe [BT] Sanhedrin 96a (649–650).
"then moses anger waxed hot ...", Exodus 32:19–20.

Section XIX

For we know all that we know only through looking at the beings; therefore our knowledge does not grasp the future or the infinite. Our insights are renewed and multiplied according to the things from which we acquire the knolwedge of them. [Maimonides 2:484–485]

"sigh in silence ...", Ezekiel 24:17.
"snow-storm a top ...", reference Zohar 1:238b (3:453), Psalms 68:15.
"... nicanor gates ...", the doors for the great Eastern Gate of the Temple Court, [BT] Yoma 38a (174–175).

p.84. "iron axes shattered on the gates", [BT] Sanhedrin 96b (650–651)
"then moses & aaron ...", Exodus 24:9–11.
"& he brought out the asherah ...", 2 Kings 23:6.

p.85. "as for the angel of the covenant ...", *Malachi* 3:1–3.
"nebuchadnezzar the scribe ...", reference *[BT] Sanhedrin* 96a (649–650)
"shebna the scribe", *2 Kings* 18:37.
"rent what could not be re-sewn", reference *[BT] Sanhedrin* 60a (408)
"elisha saw it and cried ...", *2 Kings* 2:12.
p.86. "they have slain a dead people ...", *[BT] Sanhedrin* 96b (651).
"the chariots of israel ...", reference *2 Kings* 2:12.
"so elijah said unto them ...", *1 Kings* 18:40.
"the double-portion", *2 Kings* 2:9.
"thereupon elijah took his mantle", *2 Kings* 2:8.
"the conduit/of the upper pool", *2 Kings* 18:17.

Chapter XX
Furthermore one of the marvels of this parable consists in the fact that when it mentions that Satan roams especially over the earth and accomplishes certain actions, it also makes clear that he is forbidden to gain dominion over the soul, that he has been given dominion over all terrestrial things, but that he is kept away by a barrier from the soul. [Maimonides 2:488]

p.87. "skink" an African lizard, a shin of beef: also to pour out.
p.88. "the blood of the chase", reference *[BT] Bikkurim* II:8–9 (397).
"when zedekiah rebelled ...", *2 Kings* 25:1–3; *Jeremiah* 39:1–2.
"let him follow/the dream", reference *[BT] Berakoth* 55a (337& n).
"the secret pockets ...", *Scholem* 1989:227 & 228.
"the rubble of great problems", reference *[BT] Berakoth* 3b (7).
"flying demons", reference *[BT] Berakoth* 3a (7).
p.89. "once when rabbi jose ...", *[BT] Berakoth* 3a (7).
"then in the eleventh year ...", *2 Kings* 25:4.
p.90. "the sound of the grinding fell faint ...", *Ecclesiastes* 12:4; see also *[BT] Sanhedrin* 32b (204).
p.92. "starr", a Jewish deed or bond of acquittance of debt.
p.93. "then they captured zedekiah ...", *2 Kings* 25:6–7.
"now rabbi johanan said ...", *[BT] Sanhedrin* 103a (699).

Chapter XXI
Of Adam [the Sabians] say that when he left the clime of the sun, which is

in the vicinity of India, and came to the clime of Babylon, he brought with him marvellous things: among them a golden tree that grew and had leaves and branches, also a stone tree, and a green leaf of a tree that fire could not burn. [Maimonides 2:516]

p.93. "adorned with scarlet robes ...", *[BT] Shabbath* 133b (670).
p.94. "the tables are broken", reference *[BT] Megillah* 26b (158).
"written/in sikra ...", *[BT] Shabbath* 115b (566).
"eternal pillars ...", reference *Exodus* 13:21–22.
"so he wrote in his note-book ...", *[BT] Shabbath* 12b (49).
"the walls of his house", reference *[BT] Shabbath* 115a (565).
"... coppersmiths of jerusalem", *[BT] Megillah* 26a (156).
p.95. "palanquin ...", reference *Song of Songs* 3:9–10.
"the falsehood of blank pages", reference *[BT] Shabbath* 116a (571).
"the eighty five letters ...", *[BT] Shabbath* 115b (567).
"the blank spaces", *[BT] Shabbath* 116a (569).
"against the wilderness", reference *Numbers* 24:1.
"the vineyards of learning", reference *[BT] Baba Bathra* 14a (67).
"like the ridge around a field", *[BT] Berakoth* 6a (23).
"why the scrolls of the law ...", *[BT] Baba Bathra* 14a (67).
p.96. "... of/a line", reference *[BT] Menahoth* 30a (193).

Chapter XXII

Thus it has been made clear to you, so that there can be no doubt about it, that mingled stuff, the first products [of trees], and the mingling [of diverse species] were forbidden because of idolatry; and that their customs [huqqotehem], which have been referred to, were forbidden because they led to idolatry, as we have explained. [Maimonides 2:550]

p.96. "shinning light", *[BT] Kethuboth* 17a (93).
p.97. "incardinate shame", *2 Kings* 24:4.
"sortals", the concept is closely connected with issues of identity, persistence & change. Sortal/nonsortal distinctions are believed to mark a metaphysically important difference.

Chapter XXIII

But neither of the two groups understands that [the Midrashim] have the character of poetical conceits whose meaning is not obscure for someone endowed with understanding. At that time this method was generally known and used by everybody, just as the poets use poetical expressions. [Maimonides 2:573]

p.97. "in warsaw ...", Katz et. al. 2007:39.
p.98. "five voices", *[BT] Berakoth* 6b (29).
"under which she sleeps", *[BT] Kethuboth* 17a (95).
"what was taken away ...", reference *[BT] Kethuboth* 17a (95).
"historical notation ...", Katz et. al. 2007:52.
"*parashat vayehi*", that portion of the *Torah* (Genesis 47:28 to 50:26) read in synagogue that week.
p.99. "... the twelve springs of life", *Exodus* 15:27.
"then jacob called his twelve sons ...", *Genesis* 49:1–27.
p.100. "*minim*", a heretic but more specifically a Jewish Christian.
"one day rabbi yehudah ...", *Zohar* 1:217a (3:308).
"the wood that they tossed ...", *Exodus* 15:25.
"the willow of the brook", *[BT] Ta'anith* 3a (7), *[BT] Sukkah* 44a (203); Maimonides 1963:(2) 572n.
"the tale of bricks ...", *Exodus* 5:13–18.

Chapter XXIV

In a similar way whenever the cause for a story's being narrated is hidden from thee, there is a strong reason for that story. Apply to the whole matter the principle to which [the Sages], may their memory be blessed, have drawn our attention: For it is no vain thing from you. And if it is vain, it is so because of you. [Maimonides 2:617]

p.101. "... the table of kings", *[BT] Aboth* ch 6:4 (83), see also *[BT] Hagigah* 7a (33).
"like a snare", *Psalms* 69:23.
"let the watchman repair", reference *[BT] Shabbath* 104a (499).
"satan s scarlet thread", reference Maimonides 2:597, *[BT] Rosh Hashanah* 31 b (152).
"your father s grave", *[BT] Baba Bathra* 58a (234).
"steal his soul retrospectively", reference *[BT] Pesahim* 30b (140).
"deduced by analogy", reference *[BT] Hagigah* 7a (33).

"instruments of writing", reference *[BT] Aboth* ch 5:6 (63–64), & *[BT] Pesahim* 54a (264–265).
"let us sanctify", reference *[BT] Shabbath* 104b (504).
"distinguished name", (*Shem Hameforash*) *[BT]* Sotah 38a (188).
"the subsidiary names", *[BT] Baba Bathra* 14b (69).

p.102. "... the likeness itself", *[BT] Baba Bathra* 58a (233).
"here is a table ...", *[BT] Rosh Hashanah* 24a (105).
"thirteenth month prolonged", *[BT] Rosh Hashanah* 24a (105).

p.103. "that night ...", *Esther* 6:1.
"... still being written", *[BT] Megillah* 15b (93).
"... fine flour", *[BT] Megillah* 16a (94).
"honi the circle drawer ...", reference *[BT] Ta'anith* 23a (118).
"god in bonds abolished", *[BT] Rosh Hashanah* 18b (76 & 77).
"as gentle as the reed", *[BT] Ta'anith* 20b (100 &101).
"calomel", mercurous chloride used in medicine (beautiful black).

Chapter XXV

Neither the perfection of possessions nor the perfection of health nor the perfection of moral habits is a perfection of which one should be proud or that one should desire; the perfection of which one should be proud and that one should desire is knowledge of Him, may He be exalted, which is the true science. [Maimonides 2:636]

p.106. "rabbi samuel ...", *[BT] Hagigah* 5b (23).
"rabbi eleazar ...", *[BT] Hagigah* 5b (23).
"there are names ...", *[BT] Shebu'oth* 35a (204).
"our sages taught ...", *[BT] Shebu'oth* 35b (205).
"*halachah*", the final decision of the rabbis in all matters of disputed rules of conduct.
"*ashmedai* ...", *[BT] Gittin* 68a (323).

p.107. "triptolemus" a protege of Ceres who travelled the world in Ceres' chariot distributing corn to all the inhabitants of the earth. He was said to have established the *Eleusinian* festivals and mysteries in her honour. he has also been linked with Bacchus.
"timbers of cedar", *1 Kings* 6:10.
"let the earth hear ...", *Deuteronomy* 32:1–2.

p.108. "trochilus", the crocodile *or* humming bird.

"syneidesis", passing judgements on past acts: conscience.
"seven cubits", reference *1 Kings* 6:6.
"trochus", a wheel or hoop or a round medicinal tablet.
"wreckage upon wreckage", Benjamin 1999:249.
"crescasian intervals", reference to Hasdai ibn Crescas (1340–c1412) who sought to criticise and refute Maimonides.
"electrons of fire ...", reference *Ezekiel* 1:4 & 7.

p.109. "no hammer or axe ...", *1 Kings* 6:7, [BT] *Gittin* 68a (322–323).
"when ashmedai walked ...", [BT] *Sotah* 49b (266), [BT] *Gittin* 68a (323).
"*awake awake*", *Isaiah* 52:1.

p.110. "then herod ...", [BT] *Baba Bathra* 4a (10–11).
"in early may 1944 ...", Katz et. al. 2007:61.
"logaoedic", combing dactyls and trochees. Literally a prose song.

p.111. "then the children of dan ...", *Judges* 18:27–28.
"in that day ...", *Isaiah* 7:18–19.
"of the messiah ...", [BT] *Sanhedrin* 98b (665).

p.112. " the rabbis/called him ...", [BT] *Sanhedrin* 98b (668).
"but hillel ...", [BT] *Sanhedrin* 99a (669).
"apeiron", without limits – infinite quantity and progression.

afterwords

p.116. "shibbutz", Cole 2007:542–543; Stern & Mirsky 1990:26.

p.117. "*Halachah*", the law or the path that one walks.
"... Arabic Aristotelianism", reference *Freudenthal* 2005.

p.118. "... true science of the *Torah*", Straus 1963:xliv.

p.120. "ethics of ... messianic faith", Zipes 1997:702.
"... not yet have come", Handelman 1991:162.
"still arrive at any second", Benjamin 1999:255.

bibliographical sources

Primary sources

The Babylonian Talmud, 1935f, ed Rab. I Epstein, The Soncino Press, London [cited as *BT* followed by the name of the tractate].

Mishna /Mishnayoth, 1990, ed Philip Blackman, Judaica Press, Gateshead [cited as *M* followed by the name of the tractate].

Maimonides, M., 1963, *The Guide of the Perplexed*, trans. S. Pines, University of Chicago Press, Chicago [cited by volume and page number].

— 1975, *Ethical Writings of Maimonides*, ed. Raymond L. Weiss, Dover Publications, New York.

— 1993, *Epistles of Maimonides: Crisis and Leadership*, trans. Abraham Halkin, The Jewish Publication Society, Philadelphia.

Montefiore, C. G. & Loewe, H., 1938, *A Rabbinic Anthology: Selected & arranged with comments and introduction*. Macmillan & Co., London.

The Soncino Books of the Bible, 1985f, ed. Rab. A Cohen, The Soncino Press, London [cited by book; chapter; verse].

Tanakh: A new translation of the Holy Scriptures according to the Traditional Hebrew text, 1985, The Jewish Publication Society, New York [cited by book; chapter; verse].

Zohar, Pritzker Edition, 2004f, trans. by Daniel C. Matt, Stanford University Press, Stanford, [cited by volume and page number].

Secondary sources

Anidjar, G., 2002, *"Our Place in al-Andalus": Kabbalah, Philosophy, Literature in Arab Jewish Letters*, Stanford University Press, Stanford.

Benjamin, W., 1999, Theses on the Philosophy of History, in *Illuminations*, trans. Harry Zorn, Pimlico, London (pp.245–255).

Bloch, E., 1995, *The Principle of Hope*, trans. Neville Plaice, Stephen Plaice & Paul Knight, MIT Press, Cambridge, MA.

Cavafy, C. P., 2001, *Before Time Could Change Them: The Complete Poems of Constantine P. Cavafy*, trans. Theoharis Constantine Theoharis, Harcourt, New York.

Celan, P., 2001, *Selected Poems and Prose*, trans. John Felstiner, W.W. Norton, New York.

Celan, P. & Sachs N., 1995, *Correspondence*, trans. Christopher Clark, The Sheep Meadow Press, Riverdale-on-Hudson, NY.

Cole, P., 2007, *The Dream of the Poem: Hebrew Poetry from Muslim & Christian Spain 950–1492*, Princeton University Press, Princeton.

Freudenthal, G., 2005, Maimonides' Philosophy of Science in ed. Kenneth Seeskin, *The Cambridge Companion to Maimonides*, Cambridge University Press, Cambridge.

Gantz, T., 1996, *Early Greek Myth: A Guide to Literary and Artistic Sources*, John Hopkins University Press, Baltimore.

Josephus, 1981, *The Jewish War*, trans. G.A. Williamson, Penguin Books, London.

Handelman, S.A., 1991, *fragments of redemption: Jewish Thought and Literary Theory in Benjamin, Scholem, and Levinas*, Indiana University Press, Indianapolis.

Herzberg, A.J., 1997, *Between Two Streams: A Diary from Bergen-Belsen*, trans. Jack Santcross, I.B Tauris Publishers, London.

Katz, S.T., Biderman, S., Greenberg, G., 2007, *Wrestling with God: Jewish Theological Responses during and after the Holocaust*, Oxford University Press, Oxford.

Kierkegaard, S., 1985, "Philosophical Fragments", in *Philosophical Fragments/Johannes Climacus* (vol. 7), trans. Howard V. Hong & Edna H. Hong, Princeton University Press, Princeton.

Lemprière J., 1980, *Lemprière's Classical Dictionary*, Bracken Books, London.

Levinas, E., 1996, *Proper Names*, trans. Michael B. Smith, The Athlone Press, London.

— 1998, *Otherwise Than Being or Beyond Essence*, trans. Alphonso Lingis, Duquesne University Press, Pittsburgh.

— 2000, Death and Time, in *God, Death, And Time*, trans. Bettina Bergo, Stanford University Press, Stanford (2000:5–117).

Pines, S., 1963, Translator's Introduction: The Philosophic Sources of "The Guide of the Perplexed", in *Maimonides* 1963:lvii–cxxxiv.

Rilke, R. M., 1992, *Duino Elegies*, trans. David Young, W.W Norton & Co, New York.

Rosenzweig, F., 2005, *The Star of Redemption*, trans. Barbara E. Galli, University of Wisconsin Press, Wisconsin.

Samuelson, N. M., 2003, *Jewish Philosophy: An Historical Introduction*, Continuum, London.

Scholem G. ed, 1995, *The Messianic Idea in Judaism, and other essays on Jewish Spirituality*, Schocken Books, New York.

— 1992, *The Correspondence of Walter Benjamin and Gerschom Scholem 1932–1940*, trans. Gary Smith & Andre Lefevere, Harvard University Press, Cambridge, MA.

— 1972, "The Name of God and the Linguistic Theory of the Kabbalah", *Diogenes* 1972:59–80; 164–194.

— 1969, *On the Kabbalah and its Symbolism*, trans. Ralph Manheim, Schocken Books, New York.

Stern, D. & Mirsky, M.J., 1990, *Rabbinic Fantasies: Imaginative Narratives from Classical Hebrew Literature*, Yale University Press, New Haven.

Strauss, L., 1963, How To Begin To Study The Guide of the Perplexed, in *Maimonides* 1963:xi–lvi.

Vidal-Naquet, P., 2004, Against the Murderers of Memory, in *Weber* 2004a:26–38.

Weber. E., 2004a, *Questioning Judaism: Interviews by Elisabeth Weber*, trans. Rachel Bowlby, Stanford University Press, Stanford

— 2004b, Introduction: The Youngest Children of the Republic, in ed. *Weber* 2004a:1–25.

Wolfson, E. R., 1994, *Through A Speculum That Shines: Vision and Imagination in Medieval Jewish Mysticism*, Princeton University Press, Princeton, NJ.

Zipes, J., 1997, Manès Sperber Pursues the Jewish Question in "Wolyna", in ed. Sander L. Gilman & Jack Zipes, *Yale Companion to Jewish Writing and Thought in German Culture 1096–1996*, Yale University Press, New Haven, CT.

acknowledgements & thanks:

for the extraordinary vision of J. Davidson, Governing Director of *The Soncino Press* & to the wondrous labours and erudition of Rabbi Dr Isidore Epstein and all the other scholars involved with and responsible for *The Soncino's* English translation of
The Babylonian Talmud.

to Judah J Slotka for his amazing index which offered me priceless clews as i stumbled through that "intricate and confusing maze" that is the **The Babylonian Talmud.**

to Rosemary for her patience, support and unwavering faith during my many *absences* within these writings

to Peter, Luke, Mo & Bushy for sharings of food, dialogues & laughters that have flowed ever since they responded to my invitation to sit *shiva* with me.

to Tony Frazer for accepting the first two sections of this work in slightly modified form for publication in *Shearsman (73/74, 2007)*

to all those members of the *Plymouth Language Club Discussion Group* for their generous support, over the last six years, but in particular for their helpful critical responses to the "Simeon ben Azzai" text whilst it was still work in progress.

to various audience members at *Uncut* (Exeter) and *The Plymouth Language Club* for their positive responses to my readings of sections of this work

& last but not least to Richard Burns for his gentle enquiries & encouragements.

www.ingramcontent.com/pod-product-compliance
Lightning Source LLC
Chambersburg PA
CBHW031150160426
43193CB00008B/315